LIGHT FOR THE WAY

LIGHT FOR THE WAY
Daily Bible Reading Guide

NEW TESTAMENT—BOOK 3
(Luke, Acts, and Epistles)

Frank Starr

Publishing House
St. Louis

Cover photo by Robert L. Flesher

The map on page 94 is from *God's Plan Unfolds*, in the Lutheran High School Religion Series, copyright © 1986 by Concordia Publishing House.

The map on page 95 is from *Alive by Grace*, in the Eternal Word™ series, copyright © 1982 by Concordia Publishing House.

The map on page 96 is copyright © 1979 by Concordia Publishing House. It is from the Junior High Teachers Packet in the New Life in Christ lessons.

Scripture quotations, unless otherwise indicated, are from *The Holy Bible: NEW INTERNATIONAL VERSION*, © 1973, 1978, 1984 by the International Bible Society. Used by permission of Zondervan Bible Publishers.

Library of Congress Cataloging in Publication Data
(Revised for volumes 3 & 4)

Starr, Frank.
    Light for the way. New Testament.

       Contents: bk. 1. Matthew and Epistles—bk. 2. Mark and Epistles—bk. 3. Luke, Acts, and Epistles—bk. 4. John, Epistles, and Revelation.
      1. Bible. N.T.—Reading. 2. Bible. N.T.—Introductions. I. Title.
BS2330.2.S73 1987   225.6'1   87-9050
ISBN 0-570-04482-0 (pbk.: v. 3)
ISBN 0-570-04483-9 (' : v. 4)

1 2 3 4 5 6 7 8 9 10 IB 96 95 94 93 92 91 90 89 88 87

PREFACE

Reading the Scriptures from cover to cover is very much like making a world tour to see how it all fits together and to plan for subsequent visits to certain places where the traveler can spend more time.

On that first trip through the pages of Sacred History (His-story), it is ideal to have a knowledgeable guide, even though one could get much out of taking the trip alone. The Ethiopian treasurer reading Isaiah expressed such a need to the evangelist Philip: "How can I [understand what I am reading] unless someone explains it to me?" (Acts 8:31).

Light for the Way is a daily personal Bible reading guide that takes the reader from the first chapter of the Old Testament through the last chapter of the New in designated daily stages, covering the ground in the course of two years. One can begin the trip at any time since the readings are not dated by calendar months and years.

Reading the Bible from beginning to end is a laudable goal, and everyone who can read should do so at least once in a lifetime. And the Christian has several compelling reasons for doing so.

First of all, the God whom he or she has come to love because of Christ has given this loving revelation of Himself and in it speaks to His beloved children. We get to know God and His will for us and for the world in His holy Word. And there we find treasures from the hand of a loving Father: sustenance for faith and hope, encouragement and comfort, and a storehouse of promises waiting to be claimed for our peace and joy.

The guide for this trip is Pastor Frank Starr, who accompanies the reader with appropriate comments on the background and application of each day's tour segment. The guidebook also contains introductions to the Biblical books as well as prayer suggestions and a special insight for the day.

So join those who have taken the trip before or who are taking it for the first time, or meet weekly to share discoveries. And may the Holy Spirit bless your journey!

The Publisher

5

LUKE

Wonderfully, for the Bible reader, each of the four gospels has its own individual character. Although Matthew, Mark, and Luke largely share the same general outline, each gospel (including John) makes its own contribution to our knowledge of the Lord's ministry, which culminates in His sacrificial death and victorious resurrection. Each gospel provides insights we need for a full understanding and appreciation of our Savior's work.

Certainly Luke's gospel has characteristics that have made it the favorite gospel of many Christians. From a formal literary point of view, this gospel is perhaps the most polished. Apparently written primarily for Gentiles, Luke follows the conventions of Greek literary style, beginning with a formal dedication. Although "Theophilus" may be translated "one who loves God" and be understood as a symbolic reference to the Christian reader generally, there is no reason to doubt that the "most excellent Theophilus"

was a real person, perhaps a prominent man who assisted in the production or distribution of the gospel (as Greek patrons often did).

Certain theological accents distinguish this gospel. One such accent is a consistent—and persistent—emphasis on the grace of God that accepts sinners on the basis of the Savior's redeeming work. Another accent is the universal reach of this grace that enfolds Gentiles as well as Jews, women as well as men, the poor as well as the wealthy, the rascals as well as the upright.

These and other theological emphases of the gospel accord well with an author who was a colleague of Paul, the apostle to the Gentiles, who trumpeted justification by grace through faith. Although Luke is not mentioned by name in the gospel (or in the Book of Acts), his authorship has received nearly universal acceptance in the church from earliest times.

Week One

TWO CHILDREN

The Light **Find similarities** and dissimilarities in the events leading up to the births of John the Baptist and of Jesus.

Read Luke 1.

The Lord's hand shows itself clearly in the two blessed events recorded in this first chapter of Luke's gospel. The pregnancies both of Elizabeth and of Mary superseded nature, since Elizabeth was past the time of childbearing and Mary had had no sexual relationship. The archangel Gabriel is one of two angels (Michael is the other) whose names are revealed to us. He was sent to Daniel to disclose the meaning of visions God had given to the prophet (Dan. 8:16; 9:21). Now Gabriel appears both to Zechariah and to Mary to announce the forthcoming births of their sons. In both instances God Himself gives the names of the children ("John" means "God is gracious"; "Jesus" means "God is salvation"). The Holy Spirit inspires prophetic songs of Mary and of Zechariah. Both songs (which Christians still sing in worship) are particularly rich in voicing Old Testament hopes. The song of Mary is so similar to the prayer of Hannah (1 Samuel 2:1–10) that Mary may have been consciously recalling it. Zechariah's song affirms the fulfillment of messianic prophecy and refers to John's role as the forerunner of the Messiah

The Way **With their similarities,** the parallel accounts of the births of John and of Jesus also have their contrasts. For example, compare the two receptions given to Gabriel's messages. Both Mary and Zechariah questioned how Gabriel's words could be fulfilled (vv. 18 and 34), but Zechariah's question showed doubt in the old priest's heart, causing Gabriel to impose a period of silence as a penalty. The angel's disciplinary measure accomplished its purpose, for when Zechariah next spoke, it was in worship and in prophecy.

Mary received the angel's startling announcement in trusting faith. In this way she sets a pattern for the child of God. "I am the Lord's servant. May it be to me as you have said." May we all echo her response.

The Prayer **Pray today** for faith that receives God's Word without doubting it.

The Insight **God's power** seems most effective where human limitation seems most evident.

THE SAVIOR COMES

The Light How do the events recounted in this chapter portend the nature of the Savior's mission?

Read Luke 2.

Humility and service mark the Savior's career from its beginning. The Lord of heaven and earth is born in humble circumstances, unnoticed and pushed aside by the world He came to save. The place and circumstances of His birth seem to be dictated by the policies of a Gentile government. Documents discovered in Egypt suggest that the Roman government there customarily took a census every 14 years. Luke tells us that this particular census was universal; its purpose was to enable the government to make certain that no eligible person escaped the taxes it levied. Augustus was emperor from 31 B.C. to A.D. 14. The time when Quirinius served as governor of Syria is less certain. Only shepherds, at the instigation of angels, came that day to honor the newborn Savior. Shepherds were a despised class, despite the prominence given to shepherding in the Old Testament (as, for example, in Ps. 23 and Ezek. 34).

The Way "Born under law, to redeem those under law, that we might receive the full rights of sons"—so Paul spoke of Jesus' obedience for our sake (Gal. 4:4–5). That obedience to the Law began when, according to Old Testament practice, Jesus was ceremonially "redeemed" as the first-born and His mother was purified after childbirth (see Ex. 13:1–16 and Lev. 12:1–8 for background). Mary and Joseph did "everything required by the Law of the Lord." Furthermore, when Jesus reached the age of 12, when a Jewish boy becomes a son of the Law, He joined His parents in observing the Passover in Jerusalem. (This feast of salvation would be the first and several years later the last feast observed by Jesus in Jerusalem.)

An obedient son of His heavenly Father, Jesus was also an obedient son of Joseph and of Mary. He fulfilled the Law perfectly on our behalf—both the ceremonial law, whose jurisdiction ceased with the completion of Jesus' sacrifice for our justification, and the moral law, which continues to express the Lord's will for our behavior.

The Prayer Pray today, thanking Jesus for His perfect obedience to the Law for our sake.

The Insight The Christmas spirit lives year-round in Christian hearts.

A PROPHETIC MINISTRY

The Light Make up (mentally or on paper) a fact profile on the ministry of John the Baptist as you read.

Read Luke 3.

Though brief, Luke's summary of the ministry of John the Baptist is helpful. Luke pinpoints John's ministry chronologically, using references that would be clear to his contemporaries, though not so exact to us. (John received his call sometime between A.D. 26 and 29). Furthermore, Luke demonstrates the divine origin of John's work by using a phrase ("the Word of God came to ...") often found in the Old Testament to introduce a prophet's call to service (cf. 1 Kings 12:22; 1 Chr. 17:3; Jer. 1:4; Hos. 1:1; Jonah 1:1). Luke also cites Is. 40:3–5 to point to the role of John as the forerunner of the Messiah.

Several vignettes by Luke give us the flavor of John's prophetic preaching as he led sinners to be baptized for the forgiveness of their sins. In doing so, John prepared the way for his divine successor, drawing attention away from himself, shifting the spotlight to the coming Christ. Luke tells us how Herod Antipas ended John's ministry with imprisonment. Luke later tells us indirectly that John was executed in prison (9:7–9). But Luke brings John's ministry to its climax by telling us about the baptism of Jesus, when the Savior identified Himself with sinners and started on the way that would lead Him to the cross.

The Way Two genealogies are supplied for Jesus in the gospels—here in Luke and in Matt. 1:1–17. Luke begins with Jesus and traces Joseph's line back to Adam, so indicating that Jesus had come to save all humanity. Both Matthew and Luke trace Joseph's descendants rather than Mary's, since Joseph was legally (though not biologically) Jesus' father. The differences between the two genealogies have not, so far, received a fully satisfactory explanation. Neither is complete (both are highly schematic). Luke may be emphasizing physical descent while Matthew may be tracing Christ's royal descent. Matthew, in any case, is summarizing the history of Israel and demonstrating that Jesus is the fulfillment of the promises made to Israel of the coming Messiah, while Luke stresses that Jesus came to be the Savior of all.

The Father and the Spirit joined in testifying to Jesus as the Son of God and the divinely accredited Savior. Believers also join the heavenly testimony in acknowledging Him.

The Prayer Pray today for the same spirit of repentance and of expectation that excited John's hearers.

The Insight A repentant heart prompts responsive behavior.

Week One

Thursday

THE AUTHORITATIVE WORD

The Light **Look for instances** that underline the authority of God's Word (including the Word of Jesus) as you read.

Read Luke 4.

Jesus came in fulfillment of the Word of God. The authority of God's written Word came through as Jesus cited the Word repeatedly in His confrontation with Satan. Finally, even the devil appealed to the authority of God's Word (but in a cynical, self-serving manner), though Jesus corrected his misapplication of Scripture. After the period of temptation in the desert, Jesus began his ministry of teaching. "He taught in their synagogues," including the synagogue at Nazareth where Jesus had worshiped and had heard the Word of the Lord read and expounded many times as a child and youth. Now He was reader and expositor, choosing Is. 61:1–2 as His text. He received approval initially—"all spoke well of Him." But when His exposition took a pointed turn and exposed the unbelief of His hearers ("Isn't this Joseph's son?"), Jesus aroused the anger of the congregation, which nearly executed Him for blasphemy. (They prepared to stone Jesus by first pushing Him backward from a precipice, then finishing Him off by throwing large rocks down on Him; see Lev. 24:13–16.)

The Way **By miraculous signs** (such as driving out demons and healing the sick) Jesus backed up the authority of His teaching. When the signs so astonished some that they were distracted from the Word, Jesus withdrew, for He wished people to hear the Word of God He taught. The Word alone has power to convert the hearts of sinners so that they turn and believe the Gospel. Miracles by themselves, no matter how astonishing, will convert no one; they can only back up the Word.

So it is today that the Word of God remains primary in the work of Christ's church. The Word alone can convert sinners and nourish faith.

The Prayer **Pray today** for those who preach and teach the Word of God in your congregation—your pastor(s) and the teachers of Sunday school, Bible classes, and (if you have one) Christian day school.

The Insight **Even Scripture's Lord** bound Himself to what "is written."

RESPONSES

The Light

Who responded in faith to Jesus? Who disbelieved and opposed Him? Note the answers to these questions as you read.

Read Luke 5.

Jesus revealed Himself to the fishermen Simon, James, and John by causing many fish to be caught in their nets. As experienced fishermen, they recognized that this catch was no ordinary occurrence, nor was it fishermen's luck. No doubt they had paid attention to what Jesus had taught from the shore and from the boat. No doubt also, they had heard earlier of what Jesus had said and done. They were willing, as a result, to let down their nets "because you say so," despite what their expertise as fishermen told them. And when they saw the results, they recognized the catch as a miracle. Peter's response, moving from respectful "Master" (v. 5) to worshiping "Lord" (v. 8), and his confession as a sinner show that he knew himself to be in the presence of the Lord. "Don't be afraid," the Lord assured him. "From now on you will catch men."

The Way

Though viewed with suspicion and hostility by Pharisees and teachers of the Law, Jesus found an enthusiastic reception among the outcasts and the desperate. A leper, isolated by his disease, cried out in faith and felt Jesus' healing touch. A paralytic, cared for by a small brotherhood of faith, experienced healing of soul and body by the Lord's authoritative command. Tax collectors—social and religious outcasts because of their perceived betrayal of Judaism and their close, defiling contact with Gentiles—enjoyed the forgiveness and fellowship of the Great Physician. We also can rejoice that Jesus came for the spiritually sick and to call sinners to repentance.

This company of faith knew that a new era had arrived with Jesus the Messiah. What had been appropriate behavior previously was appropriate no longer. The requirements of the old covenant should give way to the celebrative spirit of the new covenant.

The Prayer

Pray today, thanking Jesus for forgiving your sins and for calling you by the Gospel into His kingdom.

The Insight

New gifts deserve new wrappings.

Week One

Saturday

THE MESSENGERS

The Light Compare the message of Malachi to that of John the Baptist as you read.

Read Malachi 3—4.

We see connections between the prophetic figure whose ministry is recorded on the last pages of the Old Testament and the prophetic figure whose brief but explosive career is found in the first pages of each of the gospels. The first and last verses of today's reading point us directly forward to the work of John the Baptist. Jesus Himself quotes Mal. 3:1 and identifies the "messenger" in that verse as John the Baptist (Matt. 11:10—11). (The "messenger" of Mal. 3:2 is Jesus Himself, the Messiah.) In a clear reference to Mal. 4:5—6, John's father, Zechariah, points to its fulfillment in his son (Luke 1:17), an assertion that Jesus confirms (Matt. 11:14). Like Malachi, John preached a call to repentance and a need to be reconciled to God. Both prophets proclaimed that message in specific and personal terms. Malachi accused the Israelites of his day of a lack of trust that showed itself in their giving and in their speech. John warned of sins such as false pride, greed, and extortion. Both spoke of coming judgment and of the severe punishment of the wicked.

The Way And both Malachi and John pointed to the coming Christ and to the decisive importance of receiving Him in faith and obedience. Those who receive the Messiah in faith will enjoy the Lord's grace and share in His victory (Mal. 4:2; Luke 3:3), but those who oppose Him will know his burning judgment (Mal. 3:5; 4:1; Luke 3:9). The result of the Messiah's coming will be a purified people of God, refined and cleansed through suffering—the Savior's own suffering (Mal. 3:2—4; Luke 3:16—17).

Malachi promises that a faith and trust toward God that shows itself in obedience will be vindicated by the Lord's own grace and beneficence (Malachi 3:10—12). Do we trust God enough to obey Him? Although Christians are not required to tithe as were those who lived under the old covenant, are we willing to trust enough in God's care and blessing to give as much? (See Luke 21:1—4.)

The Prayer Pray today for a trust in God that shows itself in generosity toward Him.

The Insight Store in your memory this passage: "It is not the healthy who need a doctor, but the sick. I have not come to call the righteous, but sinners to repentance" (Luke 5:31—32).

13

LORD AND TEACHER

The Light   **Contrast** the teaching of the Pharisees with that of Jesus as you read.

Read Luke 6.

Challenged by some Pharisees and teachers of the Law, Jesus exposes their narrow legalism. When Jesus' disciples plucked heads of grain as they walked through a field and rubbed the grain together to separate the edible kernels from the husks, some Pharisees accused them of threshing, an infraction of the Third Commandment (Ex. 20:9–10). Jesus, in response, points out that the Law may be overruled for sufficient cause, as David did when he ate bread ordinarily reserved for priests (1 Sam. 21:1–6; Lev. 24:5–9). The spirit of the Law, the reason why it was established, counts for more than the letter of the Law, which occasionally may be eased. He who made the Law, the Lord of the Law, has the prerogative to change it. Jesus upholds the Law and fulfills it, but He will not consent to the narrow legalism of those who, while pretending to be the Law's champions, actually empty it of its goal and significance—its spirit.

The Way   **Contrast** the teaching of his opponents to Jesus' sermon on the plain. The Master Teacher begins with pronouncements of blessing on those who suffer now for the sake of God's kingdom and of woe on those who are concerned only for themselves in this life. Jesus instructs His disciples to be like their heavenly Father, who is "kind to the ungrateful and wicked" and who is merciful. Conscious of their own dependence on their Lord for mercy and blessing, disciples are to speak forgiveness, not condemnation. The disciple's life and words will flow out of a heart that has stored up the Lord's grace and love flowing into it. What a contrast between the generous, gracious spirit engendered by the teaching of Jesus and the stingy, judgmental attitude of His opponents!

Jesus' teaching provides a solid foundation for life—but only as it is put into practice. Hearing the word of Jesus, even thinking seriously about it, will do no good if we do not practice what we hear.

The Prayer   **Pray today** for those who teach the Word of God in the churches of your community, that they may faithfully transmit the spirit as well as the letter of that Word.

The Insight   **Even more important** than going to church is being the church.

Week Two

Tuesday

PRAISEWORTHY FAITH

The Light

Notice the people we meet in this chapter. How do they regard Jesus?

Read Luke 7.

Diverse groups come to Jesus' attention. The first, some Jewish elders, represents a Gentile military officer. (A centurion was in charge of a contingent of 100 men). Jesus Himself does not meet the officer but receives communications from him through others. Since the centurion was the benefactor of a synagogue, he apparently believed in the God of Israel even though, as a Gentile, he was excluded from full participation in worship or community life. Jesus praises the centurion's evident faith (expressed in terms familiar to a military man) and rewarded it by granting his request. Second, Jesus meets a funeral procession for the only son of a widow. His compassion (no one requested His intervention) moves Jesus to comfort the widow and restore her son. Finally, while Jesus is the dinner guest of Simon, an unbelieving Pharisee, an unnamed woman, moved by deep gratitude for the forgiveness of her sins, anoints and honors the Lord. Jesus uses the event to contrast the woman's faith and love with Simon's own cool detachment. The Lord commends the woman and admonishes Simon for his rude and unresponsive behavior toward Jesus.

The Way

Still another figure appears among this gallery—Jesus' own cousin and forerunner, John the Baptist. Earlier, Luke had reported that Herod Antipas had imprisoned John (3:19–20). Later, he will inform us of John's execution while in prison (9:7–9). Now we hear of messengers sent from John (probably by this time imprisoned) to ask whether Jesus is actually the Messiah. In view of John's previous confession of Jesus as the Christ (John 1:29–34), such a question may seem surprising. Perhaps, as a man with a weak and sinful nature like our own, he was now being plagued by doubts or discouragement. Or perhaps he wanted his disciples to hear the Gospel from Jesus' own lips. In any case, the Lord praises John and accredits the Baptist's unique ministry.

People today also can be chronic complainers (vv. 31–35). The Lord Himself cannot please them, far less His imperfect servants. In the end, however, self-centered grumbling will be silenced. Therefore, we raise our voices in worship, not in whining.

The Prayer

Pray today for a faith that Jesus can praise.

The Insight

Not our pedigree but our pleas appeal to the Lord.

Week Two
Wednesday

A PARABLE AND POWERFUL DEEDS

The Light **Why do not all** who hear the Gospel believe it? Watch for the answer as you read.

Read Luke 8.

Some might see a paradox (seemingly incompatible truths) in this chapter. On the one hand Jesus, the Son of God, can exercise amazing power. The disciples witness His power over the forces of nature. "He commands even the winds and the water, and they obey him." A human being might be able to sway people with his words and force of personality. But wind and water are unaffected by words—unless those words are the command of the Creator. Jesus also can command demons, those malignant subordinates of Satan. They recognize Him as the Son of the Most High God, acknowledge His eventual victory, and obey His direction. Finally, Jesus shows His power over disease and even death. A woman whom no medical practitioner could help draws on Jesus' power (even without His consent), and her illness is instantly quelled. More amazing, the life that had left a girl's body returns to it at Jesus' command. What power—power that can only have a divine source—is in Jesus' hand!

The Way **Yet people can resist** the Word of the Lord even though nature, demons, and death cannot. Jesus parable' explains why some who Hear his Word do not receive it. Various reasons are put forth—the devil steals the Word away, or people do not let the Word take root, or they allow concerns for this world's cares or pleasures to crowd out the Word. Whatever the reason, God's Word (irresistible in some quarters) can be resisted by people—not because we are more powerful than God, but because He will not force Himself on us. He desires to be loved. And love must be given; it cannot be forced.

Jesus pleads with us to hear the saving Word He addresses to us. "Consider carefully how you listen." Those who reject it lose the Word and all its benefits. Those who receive Jesus' Word and put it into practice are joined to Him in the closest possible relationship.

The Prayer **Pray today** for a heart that proves to be "good soil," one that yields a fruitful crop.

The Insight **The Lord** is a prodigal farmer. He broadcasts the seed of His Word indiscriminately, hoping for a crop.

DISCIPLESHIP

The Light **Jesus' disciples** figure in every incident recorded in this chapter. Keep your mind on the disciples of Jesus as you read.

Read Luke 9.

The disciples of Jesus were named in 6:12–16. Jesus' ministry before His crucifixion had as a primary purpose the preparation of the disciples for their later work as apostles. Their training for their coming apostolic ministries is particularly apparent in this chapter, which begins with a commission that sends them into the villages to proclaim by word and deed the arrival of God's kingdom in Christ. Their circumstances on this tour teach them to rely completely on God for their needs. That they may be confident that God will provide for them is underscored by Jesus' miraculous feeding of the 5,000. In their Lord, Jesus' disciples have all that is needed to sustain them. Jesus then draws from them a confession of their faith in Him as the Christ of God.

The Way **Immediately after** their confession, Jesus reveals to the disciples that He will suffer, be rejected, die, and be raised. He repeats this revelation shortly afterward (v. 44). On the mountain where Jesus is transfigured, He, Moses, and Elijah discuss "His departure, which He was about to bring to fulfillment at Jerusalem." Again and again and still again the Lord impresses on the disciples that He has come to lay down His life to accomplish His mission. Furthermore, He warns the disciples that they also must take up a cross to follow Him and lose their lives for Him. Redemption and victory will be won by laying life down, looking for God to lift it up once again. But the disciples are slow learners. Given authority to drive out demons (v. 1), their weak faith makes them unable to deliver a boy from demonic tormentors. They argue about preeminence. And they are quick to take vengeance.

Following Jesus is no mere Sunday afternoon excursion. He will have nothing less than complete, overriding loyalty. Christian discipleship is laying one's life before the Lord.

The Prayer **Pray today** for yourself as a disciple of Christ, that God might strengthen you to bear your cross with complete devotion to the Lord.

The Insight **Christian discipleship** is a matter of death and life.

A RECEPTION FOR THE KINGDOM

The Light **Look for instances** in this chapter where the kingdom of Jesus finds a positive reception.

Read Luke 10.

For a second time Jesus commissions followers to spread out into the neighboring towns and proclaim that the kingdom of God is near. Earlier (Luke 9:1–9) Jesus sent the Twelve on this mission. Now he sends 72 others with the same instructions. They are to depend entirely on the hospitality of those whom they visit. But Jesus adds ominous words on this occasion (v. 3) and pronounces woes on His own chosen town of residence, Capernaum, and neighboring Korazin and Bethsaida because of their unbelief despite having entertained the Savior. Nevertheless, the returning emissaries are so elated by the success of their mission that Jesus must temper their enthusiasm and place their success in perspective. Still, the Lord is moved also to pray with joy for the revelation of the Gospel to these disciples, and He congratulates them on the blessing that is theirs.

The Way **Not all** received the arrival of the kingdom that the 72 announced. Especially those who prided themselves as the spiritual elite resisted the Gospel. One such "expert in the law" prompted Jesus to tell one of His best known parables, usually titled "The Good Samaritan." Our own insensitivity to the sharp feelings separating Jews from Samaritans dulls the impact of this story for us. How stinging the reference to the unneighborly behavior of the priest and the Levite—especially when the Jewish legalist had to acknowledge the superior compassion and righteousness of the despised Samaritan! Perhaps the priest and Levite "passed by on the other side" of the road because they feared the "half dead" traveler would die in their arms, thus contaminating them and preventing them from carrying out their temple duties. (See Lev. 21:1–4.)

Jesus' gentle rebuke delivered to Martha also points up the importance of receiving God's kingdom, which is present with us in Jesus. For another look at Jesus' relationship with Martha and Mary, read John 11:1–44.

The Prayer **Pray today** for missionaries, commissioned by the Lord to bring the Good News of God's kingdom to people near or far, that they may experience joy in their work.

The Insight **Being known** in heaven is better than being famous on earth (v. 20).

Week Two

Saturday

A CHOICE TO LIVE OR DIE

The Light What would determine whether the Israelites enjoyed blessings or suffered a curse?

Read Deuteronomy 28–30.

Moses' work was nearly at an end. Soon, at the Lord's direction, he would pass to Joshua the responsibility for leading God's people. He would be permitted to gaze on the promised land but not to set foot in it. Moses would soon die in Moab, across the Jordan from Israel's destination, and God himself would bury His aged servant. But before these events took place, Moses solemnly leads Israel in renewing the covenant the Lord had made with their parents at Mount Horeb (Sinai). He charges them to keep this covenant and impresses on them the necessity of doing so. Moses speaks of the blessings that will be theirs if they keep faith with God— protection and victory over their enemies, prosperity at home and work, and the esteem and admiration of their neighbors. But if they fail to keep the covenant, the Lord will curse them. They will suffer defeat and humiliation, deprivation and desolation, suffering and great sorrow. They will even be driven from their land and scattered among the nations. Because Israel did become unfaithful to the covenant, the people did experience these horrible curses at the hands of the Assyrians and the Babylonians in 722 and 586 B.C.

The Way "Now what I am commanding you today is not too difficult for you or beyond your reach" (30:11). No one, in Moses' day or in ours, can keep the Law. From the time of the fall, all people have a sinful nature. (See Ps. 14:2–3; 51:3–5.) But the old covenant, like the new, was a covenant of grace. God put His empowering, Spirit-inspired Word "in your mouth and in your heart so you may obey it" (30:14). Furthermore, the old covenant contained provisions for atonement and restoration. Its sacrifices recognized the corruption of human nature and pointed ahead to the coming Redeemer. The apostle Paul quoted Deut. 30:11–14 (in Rom. 10:6–8) and saw in these words a reference to the Gospel.

"Choose life," Moses pleaded (30:19). Jesus came that we might have life abundantly (John 10:10). To us, too, Christ extends the Gospel and pleads, "Choose life!"

The Prayer Pray today, thanking Jesus for fulfilling God's plan revealed in the Old Testament and thanking the Holy Spirit for enabling you to choose life.

The Insight Our will to live is the work of God's Spirit.

Week Three

THE OPPOSITION ORGANIZES

The Light **Watch** for signs of gathering opposition to Jesus and note the causes of this opposition as you read.

Read Luke 11.

Not all who saw Jesus' miraculous deeds were moved closer to faith in Him as the Messiah. Some were only hardened in their disbelief. Some even dared to say that not God's power but the devil's cooperation lay behind the miracles they witnessed. Jesus refutes such an assessment by pointing out that the devil's kingdom—not God's—suffered losses because of Jesus' work. Although not actually opposing Jesus, the response of some was less than what He wanted. When a woman offered an admiring complement, Jesus called for hearing and obeying God's Word. Some sought further signs, but Jesus saw in such requests a mask for unbelief. He refused, calling for repentance like that of the Ninevites who responded to Jonah, and for attentive hearing like that given to Solomon. Jesus warns against the interior darkness of unbelief, which will not recognize God's truth spoken by God's Son. He pronounces woes on those Pharisees and teachers of the Law for whom a pious appearance was more important than repentance. Jesus assessed their influence as worse than unhelpful; it was actually destructive to the spiritual well-being of their followers. The Pharisees and teachers of the Law respond by stepping up active opposition and by seeking opportunities to entrap Jesus.

The Way **Jesus' own prayers** prompt His disciples to request, "Lord, teach us to pray." Jesus responds with the Lord's Prayer. The prayer as given here is shorter than in Matt. 6:9–13, lacking the petitions "your will be done on earth as it is in heaven" and "but deliver us from evil." This suggests that Jesus meant the prayer as a model and not necessarily as a recitation. The parable that follows emphasizes the willingness of our Father to be bothered by our frequent, persistent prayer.

"Ask . . . seek . . . knock . . . ," Jesus directs us. Are we timid about bringing our requests to our Father? He is not timid about inviting our prayers.

The Prayer **Pray today** that God the Holy Spirit will enable you both to hear and to obey God's Word.

The Insight **There are** no neutral parties in the battle between Satan and God.

Week Three

Tuesday

LIFE AS DISCIPLES

The Light **What warnings** and admonitions does Jesus give in this chapter to those who would live as His disciples? What comfort and encouragement?

Read Luke 12.

The disciple's life will not likely be an easy one. Jesus warns of external dangers: the disciple may face threats to personal safety (vv. 4–7), possible arrest and detention (vv. 11– 12), perhaps deprivation and hardship (vv. 22–25), and even hostility from within the family circle (vv. 49–53). Equally dangerous are hazards to the soul. The disciple will face the subtle, undermining influence of the attitudes of others (v. 1); a fear that confessing the Savior will meet disapproval (vv. 8–10); the temptation to think that, with the possession of wealth, we need nothing else, not even God (vv. 13–21); and the inclination to grow careless and callous while waiting longer and longer for the Lord's coming (vv. 35–48). Disciples realize that the day of judgment is coming and that now is the time to seek refuge in the reconciliation obtained for us by the Savior (vv. 54–59).

The Way **Such earnest warnings** find a ready acknowledgment from the disciple.

Nevertheless, the disciple is not left gloomy or afraid but confident and cheerful. The disciple approaches life with joy. For with His admonitions, the Lord also offers encouragement and comfort. He promises to protect and preserve His own and to give them words to speak in confession and defense. The Lord, who provides for birds and flowers, knows the needs of His disciples and will supply both physical needs and eternal possessions in heaven. The Lord will have those servants whom He finds ready and waiting at His coming "recline at the table and will come and wait on them" (v. 37).

Although we do not know the day or hour of the Savior's return in glory (Matt. 25:13), we can use our senses (and sense) to read the signs of His drawing near (vv. 54–59). Reading those warning signs will move us to repentance and faith and will fill our hearts with joy, not dread.

The Prayer **Pray today** for strength and resolve to live as a faithful disciple through good times or bad.

The Insight **The disciple's path** may be hard, but it will be solid.

TIME FOR REPENTANCE

The Light — **What is the reason** for God's patience with sinners?

Read Luke 13.

The critical hour had now arrived for Israel. For long centuries God had prepared the stage where the fulfillment of His promises would take place. God had sent prophet after prophet to warn of coming judgment, to plead for repentance, and to point to the arrival of the Deliverer from sin and destruction. John the Baptist was the last of these prophets and the herald of the Redeemer, who had now come. The kingdom of God, which the Messiah's atoning death and triumphant resurrection would usher in, was near. People could only enter that kingdom through the narrow door of repentance and faith. Little time remained to enter it. "Unless you repent, you too will all perish." God was being patient, but His patience is not unending. As the reaction of the synagogue ruler showed, many would not enter that narrow door. They had devised their own system of salvation and would have none of God's devising. The synagogue ruler represented a long line of proud Israelites whose backs were too stiff to bow before God, who had killed the prophets and stoned those sent to them. But now time was running out—"today and tomorrow and the next day." Then Jesus would crown the line of martyred prophets who died in Jerusalem, and Israel's house would be left desolate. Having rejected Jesus, it had rejected salvation and life.

The Way — **But many**—inside and beyond Jerusalem—did not reject the Lord. Though few compared to the many others, they have entered the narrow door. They have found a perch in the branches of God's kingdom.

Though rejected and belittled by the world about it, God's kingdom of grace, His church, has grown great. This has come about by the hidden power lodged in the tiny seed of the Gospel, which works like yeast, unperceived and unremarked, causing God's kingdom to come.

The Prayer — **Pray today,** thanking God for drawing you through the narrow door and into the broad expanse of His kingdom. Pray that He might use you to draw still others into His kingdom.

The Insight — **Time** is a gift with a purpose.

Week Three

TABLE TALK

The Light Three important topics that came up at a dinner are recorded in this chapter. Note these topics as you read.

Read Luke 14.

Although some of the Pharisees were out to trap Jesus, they certainly did not avoid him, nor he them. For the second time we read of dinner invitations extended to Jesus by prominent Pharisees. (See also 7:36–50.) In both of these instances the hosts were really spying on Jesus, hoping to catch Him in some compromising act or statement. Three topics of conversation came up at this dinner. The first recalled a continuing complaint—that Jesus healed on the Sabbath (see also 6:6–11 and 13:10–17). While the Sadducees (many of them priests) zealously guarded temple worship and ritual, the Pharisees (most of them laymen) zealously guarded observance of the Law, particularly keeping the Sabbath. But in their zeal these Pharisees—like the Sadducees in their concerns—had distorted the purpose of both the Law and the Sabbath. Their man-made rules, originally designed as a means to help keep God's Law, now became an end in themselves. In their scruples about minor human rules, they ignored the weightier matters of God's Law: mercy, justice, and love.

The Way To the dinner guests and later to the crowds that followed Him, Jesus spoke about discipleship. At the dinner, the Savior referred to those who would not accept the invitation to the heavenly banquet, who had all kinds of excuses. Jesus warned the crowds who eagerly followed Him of the cost of discipleship, as He urged them to consider its all-demanding nature. Following Him must mean giving up everything else—relationships, possessions, even life itself—and having only the Lord. To those who renounce all, the Lord returns all and more (Luke 18:28–30), but reward follows sincere renunciation.

Jesus' advice to invite those who cannot reciprocate (14:7–14) is not etiquette or rules for social conduct. He is encouraging us to exhibit the same grace (unmerited favor) toward others by which we ourselves stand and live before God.

The Prayer Pray today for those who have recently been your host or hostess at dinner, that such persons might be guests at God's heavenly banquet.

The Insight At God's table, His words are food.

23

Week Three

STORIES ABOUT BEING FOUND

The Light

Why did Jesus tell the three parables in this chapter?

Read Luke 15.

Jesus' ministry was a continuing offense to many Pharisees and teachers of the Law. The more successful that ministry was, the more offensive it became to them. These zealous defenders of the Law and teachers of Judaism contended that a person could lose salvation by not obeying the commandments scrupulously. They observed a comprehensive body of traditions and rules, codified by certain celebrated rabbis, in their attempt to keep the Law. What they themselves observed, they eagerly urged on others (Matt. 23:15). Their rigid (but selectively self-serving) legalism brought about confrontation with Jesus when He healed on the Sabbath. When Jesus dealt graciously (no doubt condoningly to the Pharisees) with people who seemed, by their lifestyle, to thumb their nose at the Law, they were infuriated. By simply eating with tax collectors (whose work put them in frequent contact with unclean Gentiles, and who were often extortioners and cheats as well) and sinners (whose life-styles disregarded or even flouted the Law), Jesus seemed to give social acceptance and approval to them. Such behavior contradicted, undermined, and threatened to nullify the influence of the righteous Pharisees.

The Way

To reveal the realities that lay behind His actions and to call His self-righteous opponents to repentance and a godly attitude, Jesus tells three parables. Each one underlines the gracious, merciful purpose of God to find lost sinners, to bring them to repentance and faith, and so to save them. Each parable reveals the joy in heaven when one sinner repents and is found. (How this joy contrasts with the muttering of the Pharisees and teachers of the Law over the same event!) In the last parable, Jesus brings the Pharisees and teachers into the story, putting their begrudging attitude into focus and pleading with them to rejoice also over the homecoming of lost sinners.

Where are we in the parable of the lost son? Do we see ourselves as the lost son or as the older brother? Probably we are somewhat in both. For we also were lost in sin and were found by God's grace. (Read Eph. 2:10.) Sometimes we too are prone to grumble when other sinners get better than they deserve.

The Prayer

Pray today that God would preserve us from the sin of begrudging to others the grace on which we ourselves depend.

The Insight

Redeemed sinners can suffer from short memories.

Week Three

Saturday

THE LAW

The Light — **How** do the Lord's instructions and the setting prepare the Israelites to receive the Law?

Read Exodus 19–20.

God's holiness separates Him from sinful humanity. Nevertheless, in His grace God chooses to purify His human creatures so that the intimacy that existed between Creator and creatures before sin entered into the world might be restored. The Lord's pursuance of this goal constitutes the story line of the Old Testament. At Sinai, the Lord takes an important step toward that goal: He enters into a covenant with Israel based on the statement of His eternal will in the Law and delivered through Moses. The Lord will make of Israel "a kingdom of priests and a holy nation" (19:6). In preparing to establish this covenant, the Israelites are to consecrate themselves by washing their clothing (to symbolize their need for cleansing from sin) and by abstaining from sexual relations (to acknowledge that their sinful nature is transmitted through conception and birth; see Ps. 51:5). The mountain that God will use as a meeting ground is to be regarded as off-limits to all except those whom the Lord specifically calls to meet Him on it. The Lord makes known His presence through fire, smoke, and the trembling ground. These instructions and manifestations are given "so that the fear of God will be with you to keep you from sinning" (20:20).

The Way — **The Ten Commandments** (Deut. 4:13; 10:4; literally "ten words") express God's eternal will for all people. They are as binding on us as they were on Israel under the Sinai covenant. Adam and Eve once obeyed the Law spontaneously, as we will in Paradise. Sin now makes us incapable of keeping the commandments, of obeying God's will. But Christ fulfilled the Law perfectly, and God credits His perfect record to our account. By sacrifices prescribed to make atonement, Israel was taught to look ahead in faith to the Savior's coming. Through the proclamation of the Gospel and the use of the sacraments, we look back in faith to the Savior's all-atoning work.

The Lord directed that Israel should build its altars of simple earth or uncut stones to make clear that no work of ours but only God's grace makes our worship pleasing to the Lord. True Christian worship—regardless of the beauty of our churches, their furniture or appointments—arises from the simplicity of our hearts (John 4:24).

The Prayer — **Pray today,** asking God to help you do His will from a grateful and loving heart, while trusting in Jesus' perfect obedience for your righteousness.

The Insight — **Store in your memory** this passage: "There is rejoicing in the presence of the angels of God over one sinner who repents" (Luke 15:10).

Week Four

THE IMPORTANCE OF BEING SHREWD

The Light **Two parables** help us to consider the power of money. What recommendation about the use of money does Jesus make in the first parable? What warning about the use of money does Jesus give in the second parable?

Read Luke 16.

The parable of the shrewd manager may trouble the Christian reader who fails to understand it correctly. Although some parables have several points of reference (for example, the parable of the sower, Luke 8:1–15), parables generally teach but one truth. Jesus interprets this parable for us and underlines its single truth when He says, "The master commended the dishonest manager because he had acted *shrewdly*. For the people of this world are more *shrewd* in dealing with their own kind than are the people of the light. I tell you, use worldly wealth [in the same shrewd fashion] to gain friends for yourselves, so that when it is gone, you will be welcomed into eternal dwellings." Jesus does not commend dishonesty but shrewdness. We can make money our servant when we shrewdly use it for the sake of God's kingdom and to further our goals as disciples and servants of Christ. This is the use of money that Jesus applauds and commends.

The Way **In the second parable** the Lord illustrates the seductive, corrupting power of wealth. Here is a man who has become not the master but the servant of his money. He has permitted his money to become his god. But it is a false, deceptive god. When he dies, his wealth cannot help him further; he must leave his fortune behind and face his judge as a man who deserves everlasting torment in hell. How much better off he would have been if he had used his money shrewdly. The opportunity to do so was at his gate in the person of Lazarus. Lazarus does find mercy and comfort at Abraham's side in heaven. (He is the only figure in Jesus' parables who is named; "Lazarus" means "God is my help.") How much better for the rich man if Lazarus had experienced that mercy and comfort from the rich man.

Having the Bible ("Moses and the prophets"), the rich man's brothers had God's most persuasive tool to lead people to repentance. For the Scriptures are the instrument of the Spirit, and the Gospel is the power of God. (See Rom. 1:16.) But even the Spirit may be spurned by sinners. Let us be quick to heed the Spirit while He pleads with us through the Word of God.

The Prayer **Pray today** for the shrewdness to use money as your servant in your own service to God in His kingdom.

The Insight **Manage** your money, or it will manage you.

Week Four

KEY WORDS

The Light **Find references** to attitudes that the Lord would see in His disciples as you read.

Read Luke 17.

Three key words for the disciple's life surface as Jesus converses with His disciples/apostles. The first is *forgive*. Life in this world is tangled in sin. The Lord warns His disciples to avoid sin, for sin brings woe. But sin touches even disciples. When sin comes among disciples, the offended is to forgive the offending brother. Such forgiveness prevents the damage caused by sin to spread further. The second word is *faith*. Faith wields power beyond its size. Even a little faith can do mighty work. But even a little faith is beyond human accomplishment. Faith is always a gift from God and is a proper subject for prayer. The third word is *duty* (or service). The Christian life is one of freely given service. No recompense or reward is expected. The Christian's sense of duty is a response to Christ's own sacrificial service for us. Although the Christian servant is not to expect reward, Christ nonetheless speaks of honoring His servants in the kingdom to come (Luke 12:37). A fourth word appears in the account of the Samaritan leper; this word is *thanks*. Christian disciples thank the Master, who has saved them from the living death of sin and condemnation.

The Way **While not stated,** still another key word for the disciple of Christ comes to mind as we hear Christ's admonition to Pharisees and disciples (vv. 20–37). That word is *vigilance*. The Christian is to be vigilant regarding Christ's coming in glory. Vigilant disciples will reject false rumors and expectations. Vigilant disciples will also be aware that Christ will come when least expected, when life is going on as usual. Then there will be no time for last-minute preparations. The vigilant disciple is in a constant state of readiness.

Natural occurrences (v. 17; see also Matt. 25:32–33 and Luke 12:54–56) are easily read by sinners, but spiritual signs are ignored. "Read the signs!" the Lord directs us.

The Prayer **Pray today** that your life might exhibit forgiveness, faith, service, thanksgiving, and watchfulness.

The Insight **What you see** is determined by where you look.

Week Four

ENTERING THE KINGDOM

The Light **What is needed** to enter God's kingdom? Watch for the answer to that question as you read.

Read Luke 18.

Two parables and some real people show us that faith is the key that opens the way into God's kingdom. The persistent widow continued to plead her case before the unjust judge because she had faith she would eventually be heard. The faith we show by persistent prayer is directed to God, who will "bring about justice for his chosen ones." The repentant tax collector showed faith in the grace of a merciful God. The Pharisee wrongly put his confidence in his own righteousness. Little children exemplify the complete dependence and trust that marks the faith of the Lord's chosen ones. These babies had to be brought to Jesus; they offered nothing of their own but only received. The rich ruler was unwilling to depend entirely on God for his support. The wealth of this world appears much more dependable to the worldly person. The blind beggar acted in faith that would not be discouraged. He was confident that Jesus the Messiah would open the eyes of the blind, as the prophets had foretold. (See Luke 7:22; Is. 29:18; 35:5.)

The Way **The faith** that opens the way into God's kingdom is directed toward Jesus, the Son of Man, who fulfilled the Scriptures when He was handed over to the Gentiles ("suffered under Pontius Pilate"—the Apostles' Creed) and was mocked, insulted, spit on, flogged, and killed, but who rose again on the third day. While all of this remained a mystery to the disciples for a time, they eventually, through the power of the Spirit, grasped the truth of what Jesus had revealed to them and proclaimed this Gospel with power.

Faith in Christ is the key that opens God's kingdom to us. As you grasp that key and use it, the door to paradise swings open for you.

The Prayer **Pray today,** thanking the Holy Spirit for calling you by the Gospel and enabling you to believe it.

The Insight **"Nothing** in my hand I bring, Simply to Thy cross I cling" ("Rock of Ages," by Augustus Toplady).

Week Four

Thursday

CHRIST COMES

The Light Find references to the ways that Christ comes as you read.

Read Luke 19.

The coming of Christ is a theme that runs through this chapter. First, He comes to Zacchaeus, the chief tax collector of Jericho. As Jericho was an important city (the winter residence of Herod the Great and of Herod Antipas, a center for the export of balsam, and a stop on an important trade route), Zacchaeus's post had made him wealthy. But his greatest gain came when Christ became his guest—in his heart as in his home. Zacchaeus's eagerness to see Jesus suggests that the tax collector had already heard much about Jesus, and the Holy Spirit had already prepared Zacchaeus for repentance and faith. The result: "Salvation has come to this house." Second, the parable of the 10 servants brings to our attention the time when Jesus will come again. His parable has a parallel in history, when, after Herod's death, his son Archelaus had sought to be confirmed as his father's heir. Though opposed by a Jewish delegation to Caesar, Archelaus became king. But the parable is more than a clever retelling of history; it refers to the fact that God the Father will affirm Christ as King of glory when He has ascended to heaven (see Phil. 2:9–11), and that Christ the King will return in majesty at the end of time and will call us to an accounting.

The Way Christ comes as King to Jerusalem; David's Son and David's Lord enters David's city. The prophets' words are fulfilled (Zech. 9:9), and the joyful cries of Jewish pilgrims approaching Jerusalem are affirmed (Ps. 118:26). What a joyful occasion! The hopes of generations of faithful saints in Israel receive vindication. If Jesus' disciples, representing these faithful saints, had not sung His praises, the stones of the city would have shouted His acclaim.

Tearfully, Jesus laments the doleful destiny of those who will not acknowledge His coming. He refers to the tragedy that Jerusalem would bring on itself—its destruction a generation later at the hands of the Romans. But that sad episode calls attention to the eternal destruction to be experienced by all—typified by the murderous men mentioned in verse 47—who will not recognize His coming.

The Prayer Pray today, welcoming Jesus into your heart.

The Insight Whoever will not have Christ as Savior must have Him as Judge.

Week Four

QUESTIONS AND ANSWERS

The Light **Questions** are asked and answers given in this chapter. Watch for both as you read.

Read Luke 20.

Opposition and hostility toward Jesus gather momentum. Powerful leaders plot to kill Jesus, but they are prevented from carrying out such a plan "because all the people hung on his words" (19:48). Efforts to discredit Jesus by trapping Him in a compromising statement (11:53–54) consistently fail. Jesus refuses to answer the demand "Who gave you this authority?" because He knows their motive for asking it. Jesus tells them as much by asking an entrapping question of His own (v. 3). The Lord will play no games, nor will He give Himself into their hands. Instead, He pronounces an incisive indictment on His opponents in the parable of the tenants. (The vineyard is Israel; the tenants are the leaders who oppose their Lord.) Jesus asks: "What then will the owner of the vineyard [God] do to them?" and answers His own question. To their horrified exclamation the Lord poses another question (v. 17), citing Ps. 118:22 to back up His judgment against His opponents. Another attempt to trap Jesus (v. 22) and so discredit Him fails miserably. Finally, the Sadducees (perhaps they were among the "leaders" of 19:47, since the Sadducees were the ruling party) join the Pharisees in the cat-and-mouse game. The Lord makes short work of their silly question (v. 33), which exposes their ignorance and skepticism. Even Jesus' opponents express awe at His deft defense.

The Way **Now Jesus** takes the offensive with a question of His own. Citing Ps. 110:1, Jesus challenges those who opposed Him (and by doing so, opposed their own salvation) to repent and confess with Scripture the affirmation that the Messiah is not only David's *son* (a human champion, like David) but David's *Lord* (a divine Savior sent to redeem Israel and all humanity from sin). This was Jesus' last appeal to those who stubbornly opposed God's kingdom to lay down their arms, to surrender, and to be saved. But they would not. They preferred the apparent advantages of this world to the promises of God.

"He is not the God of the dead, but of the living, for to him all are alive" (v. 38). Faith holds to this conviction, even when looking into a casket.

The Prayer **Pray today** for a greater readiness to listen to what Jesus says and to believe it.

The Insight **Faith is not afraid** to ask God questions nor to accept His answers.

30

Week Four

ZION'S KING COMES

The Light What conditions will the coming of Zion's king bring about?

Read Zech. 9:1–11:3.

The prophet Zechariah was associated with the prophet Haggai in rebuilding the temple after the Jews' return from captivity in Babylon (see Ezra 6:14). The first eight chapters contain a series of visions; the latter portion contains prophecies and revelations about the coming kingdom of the Messiah. Perhaps we see the keynote of these prophecies in 9:9, which Matthew (21:5) cites in regard to Jesus' entering Jerusalem in a festive procession only days before His crucifixion. Zechariah's prophecies in chapters 9 and 10 tell us how the Lord will demolish the threatening powers that surrounded Israel and Judah: Hadrach (mentioned only here); Hamath, a nation north of Syria; Damascus, capital of Syria; Tyre and Sidon, powerful coastal city-states west of Syria; and Ashkelon, Gaza, Ekron, and Ashdod, principal cities of Philistia, south of Tyre and Sidon. The circle will continue with references to Egypt and to Assyria (10:10–11) and to Lebanon. The Messiah/King will rule over all.

The Way But He will appear not at the head of a mighty army but "righteous and having salvation, gentle and riding on a donkey" (9:9). Away with chariots, war horses, and battle bow; "he will proclaim peace to the nations" (9:10). Jesus came to establish His eternal, universal reign not with human weapons or angel armies (see Matt. 26:52–54) but by destroying the power of sin through His obedient suffering and death to make atonement for all.

Zechariah describes the blessings of the Messiah's reign with agricultural images (9:16–10:1). Peace and prosperity and victory and reunion give joy to the people whom the Messiah/King will rule. We now live by faith in that pleasant kingdom. One day we will see and taste its delights directly.

The Prayer Pray today, thanking God for bringing you into the Savior's kingdom.

The Insight Store in your memory this passage: "Give to Caesar what is Caesar's, and to God what is God's" (Luke 20:25).

Week Five

FUTURE EVENTS

The Light For what reasons does Jesus tell His disciples about the events between His ascension and His return in glory? Watch for the reasons Jesus gives as you read.

Read Luke 21.

During the last days before His crucifixion, Jesus informs His disciples of what the church may expect during the period when He would be separated physically from the church on earth. He does not put these events in order but points out that some of them would begin soon and occur repeatedly during this period (v. 32). He predicts the destruction of the temple (v. 6) and the complete desolation of Jerusalem (vv. 20–24)—a catastrophe that occurred in A.D. 70. He warns of the appearance of false prophets and teachers who would attempt to deceive the church (v. 8). There will be wars and revolutions (vv. 9–10) and natural disasters and resulting misery (v. 11). Jesus' followers may expect harassment, hatred, persecution, and martyrdom (vv. 12–19). Finally, Jesus speaks of portentous signs in the heavens, causing upheaval and terror on earth and culminating in the shaking of the heavens and the coming of Jesus in glory (vv. 25–27).

The Way Three motives are displayed as Jesus informs the disciples of coming events.

First, He *comforts and encourages* the church. "Do not be frightened," He urges (v. 9). "Make up your mind not to worry" (v. 14). "Not a hair of your head will perish" (v. 18). "When these things begin to take place, stand up and lift up your heads, because your redemption is drawing near" (v. 28). Second, Jesus *advises* His disciples on how they should proceed. He counsels them not to prepare a defense when brought to trial, "for I will give you words and wisdom that none of your adversaries will be able to resist or contradict" (v. 15). When Jerusalem is besieged, the disciples are to "flee to the mountains, . . . get out, and . . . not enter the city" (v. 21). Third, Jesus *admonishes* the disciples to stand firm and so save themselves (v. 19), and above all, to watch, be alert, pray, and see that they are not "weighed down with dissipation, drunkenness and the anxieties of life" lest they be lost like others (vv. 34–36).

Before discussing these matters, Jesus observes the widow whose small offering represents "all she had to live on" and testifies to her faith in God to care for her. What do our church offerings say about us?

The Prayer Pray today for faithfulness and courage to withstand trials.

The Insight The light at the end of the tunnel of time is Christ.

Week Five

Tuesday

BETRAYAL, DENIAL

The Light — **As climactic events** occur that lead to Jesus' suffering and death, observe His disciples as you read.

Read Luke 22.

Although Jesus is at the center of the action in this chapter, His disciples are never far away. Satan enters into Judas, who agrees to betray the Master. Jesus sends Peter and John to locate the room where He shares the Last Supper with His disciples. He has "eagerly desired to eat this Passover with you before I suffer" (v. 15). They commune with the Lord. Jesus discloses that one of them will betray Him. Two disputes immediately arise—about who will betray Him and about who among them is greatest. Jesus gently rebukes them, then promises that they all will share His glory with Him. His warning to Simon is disregarded; His cautioning the disciples is misunderstood. While Jesus prays with agonized earnestness, His disciples doze. When He is arrested, one blunders, then flees with the rest. The one disciple, Peter, who has the courage to follow does not have the courage to acknowledge His relationship with Jesus. Too late, Peter remembers Jesus' warning, and bitterly weeps.

The Way — **Failures all**—not one disciple consistently stood by his Lord in His hour of trial. Yet Jesus never disowned or disavowed them. He foresaw Peter's restoration (v. 32). He praised and promised to reward them (vv. 28–30). He acknowledged them before His heavenly Father because they believed in Him, and He prayed for them (John 17:6–19). We can be glad that the disciples are exposed to us for what they were and as they were, for we can then see ourselves in them and know that Jesus, who could love and accept them, can also love and accept us. Only Judas was lost, and that was because he despaired of Jesus' willingness or ability to forgive and restore him. Though they faltered, they were restored by grace, the grace that led Jesus to give His life so that we might live in Him.

In the Last Supper Jesus dedicated Himself as a sacrifice of atonement for His disciples—those 12 and the millions since, down to and including us. His body was "given" for us; His blood was "poured out" for us. (In Old Testament sacrifices of atonement, blood was poured on the altar.)

The Prayer — **Pray today,** thanking Jesus for giving Himself as an atoning sacrifice for your sins.

The Insight — **"Grace,"** not "great," is the key word for Christian living.

Week Five

THE JUST AND THE UNJUST

The Light **What judgments** regarding Jesus are offered by those who witness the events recorded in this chapter?

Read Luke 23.

Clearly, Jesus' trial is nothing more than murder under a pretense of legality. The charade apparently fools no one. *Pilate* sees through the trumped-up charges of Jesus' accusers and three times (vv. 4, 14, 22) declares Him innocent. Nevertheless, bowing to a greater influence than justice, Pilate acquiesces and permits Jesus' enemies to use his power to impose the death penalty (the Jewish courts had no such authority at that time). *Herod,* though he had earlier sought to kill Jesus (13:31), does not use the opportunity Pilate so obligingly gives him and sends Jesus back to Pilate, ridiculed and mocked but unharmed, a move that Pilate interpreted as a declaration of innocence (v. 15). The *military officer* in charge of Jesus' execution regarded Him as innocent (v. 47). So did *one of the criminals* executed with Jesus (v. 41). Jesus' opponents knew that He was widely admired. For that reason they arrested Him at night and tried him at an early hour. By midafternoon (the sixth hour) Jesus was dead and was buried by sundown. Those who sympathized with Him were represented by the women who mourned and wailed for Him as He was led away to be crucified and who "beat their breasts" at His death.

The Way **A victim** of injustice? Yes, Jesus surely was that, but saying that is not telling the whole story. Though the sinful men who demanded and instigated His crucifixion cannot be excused for their shameful role (see 22:22), God the Father willed that Jesus suffer and die to atone for the guilt of humanity. (See 22:42; also 22:37; 18:31–33; 9:22, 44.) God Himself sent the Son of God to the cross for our sake.

"Jesus, remember me," the dying thief pleaded. This man confessed his sin ("we are getting what our deeds deserve") and looked only for mercy, just as the tax collector did in Jesus' parable (18:9–14). Repentance and faith provide the only door into Christ's kingdom, but it is a door that will always open to the one who knocks at it.

The Prayer **Pray today,** worshiping Jesus for dying to atone for your sins.

The Insight **Human injustice** and God's justice intersected on Jesus' cross.

AN EVENTFUL DAY

The Light Notice the sequence of events and their location as you read.

Read Luke 24.

None of the gospels record every postresurrection appearance of Jesus. We obtain a complete account of the 40 days after the Lord's resurrection by reading all of the gospels along with various passages from the epistles. Luke records some of these events. The gospels all tell us that faithful women were the first to find the tomb empty and to be told that Jesus had risen (vv. 1–12, 22–23). Next, Peter and another disciple went to the tomb (v. 24; John 20:3–9). Mary Magdalene and Mary the mother of James were the first to see the risen Lord as they returned from the tomb (Matt. 28:9–10; Mark 16:1, 9–11; John 20:10–18). Later that same day Jesus appeared to two disciples (not part of the Twelve) as they walked to Emmaus (Mark 16:12–13; Luke 24:13–35) and separately to Peter (Luke 24:34; 1 Cor. 15:5). That same day, Jesus appeared to the 11 disciples (Mark 16:14; Luke 24:36–49; John 20:19–23). During the next 40 days Jesus appeared to His disciples several times (1 Cor. 15:5–6), including another appearance especially for Thomas's benefit (John 20:24–31) and an appearance at the Sea of Galilee, or Sea of Tiberias (Matt. 28:16–20; Mark 16:7; John 21:1–23). Jesus' final appearance was near Bethany, a village on the Mount of Olives, two miles southeast of Jerusalem (Luke 24:50–53).

The Way Despite Jesus' repeated statements before His crucifixion that He would be crucified and on the third day would rise again, His disciples remained confused about these events until overwhelmed by the obvious. Peter returns from the empty tomb, where he has seen the discarded burial cloths, "wondering to himself what had happened" (v. 12). Jesus scolds Cleopas and his companion as "foolish" and "slow of heart to believe all that the prophets have spoken" (v. 25). Then the Lord enlightens them by explaining the Scriptural (Old Testament) attestations to the resurrection of the Messiah.

"Were not our hearts burning within us while he talked with us on the road and opened the Scriptures to us?" (v. 32). May God the Holy Spirit give us also this "heart burn" that results from the ingestion of the promises found in Scripture!

The Prayer Pray today for a more certain conviction that the Lord has risen and is alive.

The Insight Faith comes not through the eye but through the heart.

ACTS

An old title, "The Acts of the Apostles," does not adequately or even accurately denote the contents of this New Testament chronicle. Only two apostles figure prominently in the book—Peter and Paul—and Paul was not one of the Twelve. Nor is the book a history of the church in the apostolic period; it is far too incomplete for that. Even from the narrow section of the history that Acts chooses to tell, much is left out.

Acts is a demonstration of how the Gospel of Jesus made its way outward from Jerusalem through Judea and Samaria to the ends of the earth (Acts 1:8). Not the acts of the apostles but the acts of Jesus working through the Holy Spirit are the subject of this book, which might better have been titled "The Acts of Jesus" or "The Gospel According to the Holy Spirit."

Luke makes his purpose clear to us by stating a theme (1:8) and then indicating (by periodic summary statements) how this theme is carried out (6:7; 9:31; 12:24; 16:5; 19:20; 28:31). He shows us how the church grew in Jerusalem, how persecution actually caused its spread, how Gentiles also came to faith in Christ, how Jews and Gentiles were united in a brotherhood of faith, and how the Gospel extended in ever-widening circles until it reached Rome, at that time the world's capital. In giving us this account Luke provides verification of Paul's conviction: "I am not ashamed of the gospel, because it is the power of God for the salvation of everyone who believes: first for the Jew, then for the Gentile. For in the gospel a righteousness from God is revealed, a righteousness that is by faith from first to last, just as it is written: 'The righteous will live by faith' " (Rom. 1:16–17).

WITNESSES

The Light — **Why was it "necessary"** (v. 21) to replace Judas and restore the number of apostles to 12? Think about this as you read.

Read Acts 1.

Perhaps most readers consider Acts to be a history of the apostolic church. After all, doesn't the title, "The Acts of the Apostles," imply this? But is it really true that this is an account of the apostles' work? Actually, we lose sight of most of the apostles soon after Pentecost. Verse 13 is the last New Testament mention of Andrew, Thomas, Philip the apostle (another Philip occurs later), Bartholomew, Matthew, and Simon the Zealot. James is mentioned only once more, a report of his murder by Herod. (Another James, the brother of Jesus, becomes the leader of the church in Jerusalem.) This book is not so much an account of the acts of the apostles as the acts of Jesus Himself as He works through the Holy Spirit. Luke calls his gospel an account of "all that Jesus *began* to do and *teach* until the day he was taken up to heaven." The apostles will be Jesus' witnesses in Jerusalem, in all Judea and Samaria, and to the ends of the earth. Accordingly, Acts begins in Jerusalem, shows how the Gospel was taken throughout Palestine, and ends with Paul in Rome. The Word had spread out from one end of the Mediterranean world to the other.

The Way — **The Jews** were the Gospel's first target. Christ came as the fulfillment of prophecies made through the patriarchs and prophets. Although all humanity was to enjoy the redemption brought about by the Messiah, Israel—God's chosen instrument through whom the world's Savior would appear—should taste the Gospel's sweetness first. (See Rom. 1:16.) Christ chose 12 apostles to represent the mission to all Israel (which consisted of 12 tribes). Though Peter and others also proclaimed the Gospel to Gentiles, the Twelve labored primarily among the Jews. Paul was called as the apostle to the Gentiles (Acts 9:15; Rom. 11:13–14), though he also observed the evangelistic principle: to the Jews first.

"You will be my witnesses...." The apostles were witnesses to Christ's resurrection, which they experienced firsthand, but all Christians are witnesses to the Gospel, which we have experienced firsthand. We are Christ's witnesses; may God make us ready witnesses.

The Prayer — **Pray today** that the Holy Spirit might make you a more effective witness for Jesus.

The Insight — **In praying** we speak up; in witnessing we speak out.

Week Five

MEALS TO REMEMBER

The Light **How** was the annual celebration of the Passover and of the Feast of Unleavened Bread related to Israel's deliverance from Egypt?

Read Exodus 12:1–15:21.

Before God rescued Israel from slavery to the Egyptians, He established a commemoration by which the event might be remembered throughout future generations. Every aspect of this commemoration was important. The *lamb* was a central feature; its blood, smeared on the doorposts of Israelite households, spared those households from the ravage of the avenging angel that took the life of firstborn males, both human and animal, in all other households. The lamb's flesh, roasted and consumed by the Israelite family, became the bond of a communion they shared with God and one another. Eating *unleavened bread* for seven days reminded Israelites of their rescue from Egypt, when they had no time for yeast to rise as they fled the pursuing Egyptians. Another act also commemorated the days of the exodus: the redemption of the firstborn. Every firstborn male, whether human or animal, was to be regarded as claimed by the Lord, just as He had claimed every firstborn male in Egypt. Firstborn male animals were to be redeemed by a sacrifice or were to be killed to dedicate them to the Lord. Firstborn boys were to be redeemed by a prescribed sacrifice. (For the application of this rule to Jesus, see Luke 2:22–24.)

The Way **Jesus inaugurated** the new covenant under which no further sacrifices would be needed after His own sacrifice on the cross. He commemorated this redeeming event by replacing the Passover with the Lord's Supper. In place of the Passover lamb, Jesus places before us His own body given for us and His own blood shed for us. By the sacrifice of Himself, the Lord has freed us from the slavery of sin. Jesus used elements of the Old Testament commemorative meal—unleavened bread and wine—in instituting the commemorative meal of the New Testament.

Both commemorative events, Passover and the Lord's Supper, were established *before* the events they were to commemorate took place. This underlines their divine origin. With God there is no need to wait and see.

The Prayer **Pray today,** thanking Jesus for establishing the Lord's Supper and asking His help as we participate in this Sacrament thoughtfully and with faith in the promises He attaches to it.

The Insight **Store in your memory** this passage: "You will receive power when the Holy Spirit comes on you; and you will be my witnesses in Jerusalem, and in all Judea and Samaria, and to the ends of the earth" (Acts 1:8).

Week Six

Monday

A SHARP SERMON

The Light **Analyze** the proclamation of the Gospel on the occasion described here. Note the composition of the congregation, the content of Peter's address, and the results of his preaching.

Read Acts 2.

The first public proclamation of the Gospel by the apostles after Jesus' ascension is rich with implications for what was to come. The Holy Spirit set the stage for this remarkable occasion. Assembled before the apostles was a polyglot congregation coming from all directions. Parthia lay southeast of the Caspian Sea; Media was southwest of the Caspian Sea; Elam was below Media; and Mesopotamia was east of Elam—all of these areas would be northeast and east of Jerusalem (today's Iran). Cappadocia, Pontus, Asia, Phrygia, and Pamphylia were all in Asia Minor (today's Turkey), thus northwest of Jerusalem. Rome would be due west of Jerusalem, across the Mediterranean. Egypt and Libya and Cyrene (capitol of Cyrenaica) were in North Africa. (Cyrenaica is now east Libya.) Crete is an island in the mid-Mediterranean, Arabia was located southeast of Jerusalem (today's Saudi Arabia). Jewish visitors from all around were drawn to Jerusalem for Pentecost, a harvest festival seven weeks after Passover. (See Lev. 23:15–22.)

The Way **To this international audience** Peter proclaims the Gospel. (We probably have a summary of his entire address.) He starts by explaining that the phenomenon witnessed by the astonished holiday crowd was a fulfillment of a prophecy by Joel (2:28–32) that would occur at the time of the Messiah's coming. Peter identifies Jesus as the Messiah and demonstrates that His death, resurrection, and ascension were foretold in Scripture, citing Ps. 16:8–11 and Ps. 110:1. Peter's words hit their mark, cutting through the sin overlaying the hearts of his audience and exposing them to the sharpness of the truth. These convicted sinners are now ready for the comfort of the Gospel. Many are baptized.

The apostolic church devoted itself to "the apostle's teaching and to the fellowship, to the breaking of bread [quite likely a reference to the Lord's Supper—see 1 Cor. 10:16] and to prayer." Could you say that your congregation is similarly devoted?

The Prayer **Pray today** for a greater attentiveness to the Gospel as it is proclaimed in your church.

The Insight **A successful sermon** still exposes the sin, then presents the Savior.

Week Six

GETTING ATTENTION

The Light Notice how Peter and John escalate an act of compassion into a proclamation of the Gospel.

Read Acts 3.

The Lord sets the stage for two of the disciples to serve as His witnesses, beginning in Jerusalem—even within the temple. Peter and John arrive at the temple for one of two daily times of prayer (early in the morning and mid-afternoon, when daily sacrifices also took place—see Num. 28:1–8). Jewish Christians continued to frequent the temple for worship, perhaps until persecution drove them away. The temple was also a natural place for witness and teaching (Acts 5:21). Beggars (those who depended on public charity for daily needs) would naturally gather at the temple, for almsgiving was prescribed for faithful Israelites (Deut. 15:11). Peter and John had no money, but they had much more to give—the power of Jesus working through them. As the disciples responded in compassion and faith, Jesus intended their act to benefit many more people than just the beggar. Those who saw the formerly lame man "walking and jumping and praising God" were prepared for an even more significant miracle—their own conversion to faith in Christ as the Messiah.

The Way Peter's response to the astonished looks of those who saw the lame man's restoration persuasively marshals the case for receiving Christ as the Messiah. The lame man's restoration manifests the power of the glorified Christ, whom God vindicated by the resurrection. Though crucifying Jesus was a great crime, forgiveness is available through repentance. Moses, Samuel, and all the prophets plead with us to receive Jesus as Christ and Savior, the fulfillment of the promises that the Lord made through them.

Peter and John immediately directed their audience to Jesus as the one who empowered their Christian work. Do we also make certain that Jesus gets the credit for the good we do?

The Prayer Pray today for those whose Christian work attracts attention, that God might keep them humble and that they might glorify Jesus. Pray for such people by name if you can.

The Insight Christians stand behind Christ, not in front of Him.

Week Six

BOLD REPLIES

The Light Note the bold replies of Peter and John. What enabled them to answer as they did?

Read Acts 4.

So successful were the disciples in bearing witness to Jesus as the Messiah that the authorities began to grow concerned. They had recently done away with the chief troublemaker—Jesus—and had seemingly succeeded in intimidating His followers as well. But now these disciples had become bold, not afraid even to proclaim Jesus as the Messiah publicly in the temple itself. Summoned before the highest court of Judaism, the Sanhedrin, the disciples boldly declared that they would keep right on proclaiming Christ as Messiah as Jesus said they would (Luke 21:12–19). "Judge for yourselves whether it is right in God's sight to obey you rather than God. For we cannot help speaking about what we have seen and heard" (Acts 4:19–20). The Sanhedrin comprised 70 of the most venerable elders of Israel, with the high priest himself presiding. It had power to expel a person from Judaism and—when Roman authorities were absent or would look the other way—even to execute offenders. But the disciples appealed to a higher jurisdiction, one to which even the Sanhedrin must yield: the court of heaven, and to God himself as Judge.

The Way Not surprised when human authorities opposed Christ and his church, the disciples knew from Scripture that the powers of this world have often opposed God and His kingdom. They saw in the collusion of the Gentile Pilate and the Jewish Herod (at least he fancied himself a Jew, though orthodox Jews repudiated him) the fulfillment of Ps. 2:1–2. But the disciples remembered also that the psalm declares: "The One enthroned in heaven laughs; the Lord scoffs at them. Then he rebukes them in his anger" (vv. 4–5). So the church prayed (and prays) in confidence for increased boldness to proclaim the Gospel of Christ.

Compassion and generosity characterized the church in apostolic times. May the same attributes be true of our churches today.

The Prayer Pray today for Christians in lands where authorities are hostile to the Gospel, that God might grant to the church faith, courage, and boldness.

The Insight Though enemies may cruelly grasp the church by its throat, they cannot silence its voice.

PERFIDY AND PERSECUTION

The Light **From within** and without come challenges to the church's integrity. We find challenges from both directions in the reading today. Identify these challenges and note how the apostles deal with them.

Read Acts 5.

We may first think that Ananias and Sapphira receive a harsher penalty than they deserve. We might regard their offense somewhat more lightly. Even though they tried to give the impression that they were giving more than they really did, they were not required to sell their property at all, as Peter points out (v. 4). Nor were they required, having sold the property, to deliver over all the proceeds to the apostles. Peter exposes the heart of their offense when he charges Ananias with lying not merely to the church or to the apostles but to God. Confronting Sapphira, Peter charges the couple with conspiring "to test the Spirit of the Lord." Did this pair actually believe they could fool God? Denying that God could know about their scheme amounts to unbelief; deciding that God would not care about their deception amounts to blasphemy; disregarding whether God knew or cared amounts to a mockery of God. In any case, although their motives may remain somewhat unclear to us, examining the implications of their act clarifies its enormity.

The Way **To their opponents** Peter's explanation for the disciples' behavior—"We must obey God rather than men!"—states succinctly the duty of the church in a hostile world. Our course of conduct must not be charted by practical advantage or popular opinion but by obedience to the revealed will of God. Not what others may think or do but what the Lord has said and done in redeeming us will determine what we say and do. As we obey God, we will also trust Him to guide and guard us.

Gamaliel's advice provides a sample of this celebrated teacher's wisdom. Paul claims Gamaliel as his mentor. The history of Christianity has vindicated Gamaliel's conclusion.

The Prayer **Pray today** that the church in our day might rebuke error and misconduct that come from within and rebut opponents without.

The Insight **Every true witness** tells a story that fits the facts, not the circumstances.

Week Six

Friday

A DIVISION OF MINISTRY

The Light — **What brought about** an expansion of the ministry of the church?

Read Acts 6.

The Gospel ministry unfolds in the New Testament as needs develop. To this point the 12 apostles (including Matthias, selected to take the vacant place of Judas Iscariot—Acts 1:12–26) have fulfilled the needs of the church for spiritual leadership. But as the size and complexity of the church increased, the work to be done outstripped the resources available in the apostles. The apostles themselves proposed (they did not dictate) a solution that won the approval of the entire church. Seven additional workers, gifted both spiritually and mentally, were to assume responsibility for a specified part of the apostles' work, administering the distribution of food to needy Christians. (These resources were made available by the generosity described in 4:32–37.) Later, as Christian congregations grew by the missionary work of the apostles and others, God provided additional ministries and leadership posts to meet the needs of the church.

The Way — **Two of the seven** new workers named in 6:5–6 were to distinguish themselves for activities beyond the strictly administrative ones for which they were chosen. Stephen, who was particularly "full of faith and of the Holy Spirit," soon became a leading evangelist and apologist (defender) of the Gospel. But though opponents "could not stand up against his wisdom or the Spirit by whom he spoke," their frustration led them to slander and falsely accuse him, as these opponents had earlier slandered and committed perjury against Jesus. Another of the seven, Philip, also became an evangelist (8:4–7, 26– 40; 21:8–9).

"The word of God spread." Acts will repeat this or a similar phrase at 9:31; 12:24; 16:5; 19:20; 28:31 to show how the church carried out Christ's commission in 1:8. The same description applies to Christian history since. Are you and your congregation in the forefront of this advance of the Gospel?

The Prayer — **Pray today** for those (professionals and volunteers) who administer the church's work, that they might discharge their duties effectively.

The Insight — **Sharing the work of ministry** is a strategy devised by the Spirit.

BACKWARD AND FORWARD

The Light In what respect is the multiplicity of languages a mark of humanity's sinful nature?

Read Genesis 10–11.

The flood was God's judgment against the increasingly arrogant sinfulness of men and women. But the flood did not eradicate the problem of sin. Even after the flood God said of humanity, "Every inclination of his heart is evil from childhood" (Gen. 8:21). The depth of this depravity came to be seen again some time after the flood in a presumptuous act that caused God to act once more with a stroke of judgment. When God brought Noah and his family out of the ark, He commanded their descendants to "fill the earth" (9:1). But instead of obeying this command, a new generation of sinners determined to regroup and offer a united front against God. "Come, let's make bricks and bake them thoroughly. . . . Come, let us build ourselves a city, with a tower that reaches to the heavens, so that we may make a name for ourselves and not be scattered over the face of the whole earth" (11:3, 4). But God has a "Come, let us" of His own. By confusing their language, the Lord made it impossible for people to conspire, and forced them to scatter all over the earth, forming many peoples and nations, "each with its own language" (10:4, 20). (Apparently, in a time sequence, 11:1–9 precedes chapter 10.)

The Way So the diversity of language is actually a result of God's judgment and a testimony regarding the sinfulness of the fallen human nature. But if the confusion of languages is that, then the Gospel's bridging of these languages at Pentecost is a testimony to the healing of the nations that the Gospel brings about. The phenomenon at Pentecost that enables the polyglot crowd to hear the apostles "speaking in his own language" and "declaring the wonders of God in our own tongues" (Acts 2:6, 12) becomes a fulfillment of the day prophesied by Joel when "everyone who calls on the name of the Lord will be saved" (Joel 2:32; Acts 2:21). Read Paul's comment in Gal. 3:26–29 about the unity brought about by the Gospel.

The seed to the reversal of the confusion, separation, and alienation caused by sin lay in a descendant of Noah's son Shem—in Abraham, by whose Seed all nations would be blessed (Gen. 12:2–3). God would move forward despite the backward direction caused by sin.

The Prayer Pray today for peace among nations, a peace that grows out of faith in the Prince of peace by more and more people from every nation.

The Insight Store in your memory this passage: "We must obey God rather than men!" (Acts 5:29).

Week Seven

STEPHEN'S DEFENSE

The Light

How is Stephen's speech a reply to the charges made in 6:13–14?

Read Acts 7.

Stephen had been accused of maligning the temple and the Law and of promoting the views of one who had advocated destroying the temple and of altering the sacred traditions of Judaism. Were these accusations true? Stephen might have replied to the charges simply and directly. He might have pointed out that Christian Jews continued to frequent the temple for worship (2:46; 3:1) and to practice Jewish customs. He might have explained that Jesus' remarks regarding the temple had been intentionally misrepresented. (See John 2:19–22; Matt. 26:61; 27:40.) He might further have said that, far from changing, altering, or abolishing the Law, Jesus defended and fulfilled it. (See Matt. 5:17–20; Luke 16:16–17.) But Stephen could not have made such a timid, partial defense and remained true to his calling as a witness to the truth of the Gospel. Stephen had to go further than refutation.

The Way

Stephen's reply to the worn-out, trumped-up accusations made against

both his Lord and himself reversed the situation and put his opponents on trial—as, in fact, they were. Before God the rulers stood guilty of stubborn unbelief and the rejection and murder of God's own Son. (Jesus makes the same charge in the parable of the tenants, Luke 20:9–19.) Instead of being zealous defenders of the covenant given through Moses, these arrogant rulers were carrying on the criminal careers of their forefathers as rebels and outlaws against God's Law and temple. They had abused and mutilated both institutions further; they had murdered that Holy One who sanctified both Law and temple.

As Stephen's witness faithfully declared the truth of God's Word, so his prayer wonderfully reflected the grace of God's Son. (See Luke 23:34, 46.) May we be true reflections of our Lord's grace and declarers of His truth.

The Prayer

Pray today for the courage to speak God's truth faithfully, even when that truth is not wanted.

The Insight

An accusation may say more about the accuser than about the accused.

A SORCERER AND A STRANGER

The Light **Compare** the two individuals whose conversions through the ministry of Philip are related in this chapter.

Read Acts 8.

Simon, a Samaritan sorcerer became the subject of legends, and the sin of buying church offices (simony) is named after him. Simon assumed that the power of imparting the Holy Spirit through the laying on of hands is inherent in the office of bishop. In offering money for this power, Simon offered to buy this church office. Simon seems to have contradictory motives. On the one hand, he believes the Gospel and is baptized. Yet his offer to buy the power of imparting the Spirit betrays a heart that is not right before God and is "full of bitterness and captive to sin." Convicted and admonished by Peter, Simon's reply gives evidence of repentance. Peter's admonition, though pointing out the seriousness of Simon's sin, implies that forgiveness and restoration are available to him. We have no reason to conclude that Simon did perish with his money. His case reassures us that even when Christians fall into great sin, repentance and forgiveness are still possible.

The Way **Soon after,** another memorable person crosses Philip's path. This stranger to Israel, an Ethiopian court official, like many Gentiles, had come to faith in the God of Israel. He exhibits that faith by his coming to Jerusalem to worship and by his interest in the Bible. Philip uses the Bible to bring him to see and accept the fulfillment of Israel's faith in Jesus as the Messiah. Philip used Is. 53:7–8, one of the "Servant Songs," to show that Jesus had fulfilled the promises found in the Old Testament.

Two dissimilar people, a Samaritan sorcerer and an Ethiopian official, both came to know the grace of God in Jesus. We also, though similar in some ways and different in others, share with all Christians our salvation by grace through faith.

The Prayer **Pray today** that you may be preserved from sin that threatens your salvation.

The Insight **Money** has never bought passage to heaven but often to hell.

A SURPRISING CONVERSION

The Light Why did Ananias hesitate to follow orders and go to Saul?

Read Acts 9.

That Saul would become a Christian missionary must certainly be among the more surprising conversions of all time. Saul was a zealous persecutor of Christians, one whose fanaticism saw virtue in killing his opponents. Going over to the other side must surely have been the farthest thing from his mind as he started out for Damascus. His background had prepared him for leadership in Judaism. Though born in Tarsus of Cilicia (in southeast Asia Minor), he grew up in Jerusalem, where he received a thorough training in Jewish law under the renowned Gamaliel (Acts 22:2–3). He became a Pharisee (26:5) and soon distinguished himself for his zeal as an enemy of "the Way." (A name used by Christians themselves to refer to their faith, the name "the Way" occurs only in Acts. The term apparently gave way to "Christians," a name first applied by outsiders—see 11:26.) No one was more surprised at Saul's conversion than Saul himself—unless it was the church (9:21). Saul (or Paul, as he is better known to us) credits his conversion entirely to God's gracious choice (1 Cor. 15:8–10).

The Way Once converted, Saul begins to share his newly received conviction "that Jesus is the Son of God." Having left for Damascus to root out faith in Jesus as the Christ, he arrives to become its most powerful and effective advocate. From his own writings we learn (Gal. 1:15–24) that, after fleeing Damascus, he spent a period of time in Arabia and then returned to Damascus. After a three-year ministry there Saul went to Jerusalem, where he met Peter and James. When his life was endangered in Jerusalem, the church sent Saul to Tarsus by way of Caesarea. There he lived quietly for years (2:1). We next find him serving as a minister of the church at Antioch (Acts 13:1).

A Christian woman, Tabitha (an Aramaic name, which in Greek is Dorcas), had commended her faith to many through her good works during her life. But her death became the occasion of an even more effective witness when Jesus raised her from death through the ministry of Peter. How wonderful if we, in life and in death, might be instrumental in causing others to believe in Christ.

The Prayer Pray today for someone you know (or know of) who does not appear to believe in Jesus as Savior, that God might bring him or her to faith in Christ.

The Insight God's grace may be surprising.

LEAPING A BARRIER

The Light What means did God use to bring Cornelius and Peter together? Why was it necessary for the Lord to go to such lengths?

Read Acts 10.

Already the availability of the Gospel to Gentiles as well as Jews has become clear. Philip baptized Samaritans and an Ethiopian. The Lord has called Saul that he might be commissioned "to carry my name before the Gentiles and their kings and before the people of Israel" (9:15). Now He takes a direct hand in bringing together a Roman military officer and the apostle Peter so that the apostle might incorporate Cornelius and many other Gentiles into the church. But why was it necessary for the Lord to send an angel to Cornelius, a believer in the God of Israel, and to provide a special vision for Peter to bring about this preaching date for the apostle? Peter's response to the Lord's command, "Get up, Peter. Kill and eat," suggests the answer. For generations Jews had been trained to avoid close contact with Gentiles (v. 28). This was necessary to preserve the people of Israel as God's chosen instruments through whom He might bring forth the Messiah, the Christ, to be the world's Savior.

The Way But now this "barrier, the dividing wall of hostility" (Eph. 2:14–18) was no longer needed. The Lord would take it down, making Gentiles "fellow citizens with God's people and members of God's household" (v. 19). But this step was not easy for Jews like Peter, in whom separation from Gentiles had become nearly instinctive. Throughout the apostolic period the struggle to integrate Jews and Gentiles into one fellowship continued. It has not ceased to this day; only the slowing of Jewish conversions to a mere trickle has eased tensions caused by Jewish-Gentile integration into the church.

God's people still must fight against the tendency to make distinctions based on race, class, and economic status. Paul's affirmation in Gal. 3:26–29 remains an unrealized goal.

The Prayer Pray today for a greater sense of brotherhood and unity among Christians.

The Insight All tickets into God's kingdom are first class.

Week Seven

Friday

A CHURCH FOR GENTILES

The Light What response did Peter give to those who complained that he had violated a divine command separating Jews from Gentiles? What resulted from Peter's explanation?

Read Acts 11.

God enlightened Peter about His will to bring the Gospel to Gentiles and to receive them on an equal basis into His kingdom. But Peter's colleagues were yet to be enlightened, and they objected to Peter's behavior among Gentiles. Peter's response to their indignant charges is neither defensive nor angry. He calmly fills them in on what had happened, enabling them, too, to benefit from the Spirit's revelation to him. He recalls what the Lord had said about receiving the Holy Spirit (vv. 16–17). Those who heard Peter's explanation draw their own conclusions. The whole episode reflects credit on Peter and on those who first criticized him. May we take the same approach when we are upset about something done in the church.

The Way We resume the story of Saul, whom we left at Tarsus in Cilicia (9:30). Barnabas, who had befriended Saul when all others suspected him (9:27), once again seeks him out in Tarsus, adopts him, and draws him into pastoral work in Antioch of Syria. Barnabas first appears at 4:36–37, where we learn that his proper name was Joseph, that he was "a Levite from Cyprus," and that he sold property and gave its proceeds to the church to provide for its needy members. The name the apostles gave him (Barnabas means "Son of Encouragement") describes his character. Barnabas accompanied Saul on the first missionary journey, but disagreement separated them as they began the second journey, with Barnabas and Mark going to Barnabas's native Cyprus. Later references both to Mark and to Barnabas (1 Cor. 9:6 and 2 Tim. 4:11) assure us that the quarrel did not permanently separate Saul from this "good man, full of the Holy Spirit and faith" (Acts 11:24).

Though Antioch was (at least partly) a Gentile congregation, the Christians displayed a love that transcends ethnic and racial barriers when they assisted needy Jewish Christians in Judea. This act of charity was later repeated by the churches in Greece. May the same charitable spirit move us to share with needy Christians in other lands.

The Prayer Pray today for the realization of harmony and brotherhood among Christians of different races.

The Insight What an honor to be known as a "Christian," one who is associated with Christ.

Week Seven

THE SERVANT WHO SAVES

The Light — Who is the speaker in the first seven verses of this chapter?

Read Isaiah 49.

The first half of the chapter is among the "Servant Songs" of Isaiah. The other such songs occur in 42:1–9; 50:4–9; and 52:13–53:12. As we read these passages, we perceive that Isaiah is referring beyond himself or Israel to one whom God identifies as "my Servant." The identification of this Servant as Jesus comes as no surprise to the Christian reader, who easily recognizes the features of his Savior in these passages. But the New Testament citations clinch the matter. Paul relates 49:6 to Jesus in Acts 13:47 and refers to this passage also in 26:23. As Paul declares, Isaiah's prophecy in this chapter shows that Jesus came into the world to save not only Israel but the Gentiles as well. Though this truth is particularly proclaimed by Paul (both in his sermons in Acts and in his epistles), Jesus' role as Savior is revealed throughout the New Testament and in many places in the Old Testament as well.

The Way — God promises in this chapter to respond to the hopes of His people and to save them. Actually, two levels of salvation are apparent. God will save Israel from its captivity in Babylon and restore the people to their land. He will drive away Israel's conquerors, and exiled and refugee Israelites will return to their land in such numbers that it will not be able to contain them. This deliverance did occur. But the redemptive event, the return from exile, is a precursor of a far more important redemption—the salvation of all nations, including Israel, from captivity to sin and exile from God's kingdom. As God effected Israel's return from captivity in Babylon, so He has also effected the salvation of all from slavery to sin.

God acts on a grand scale, exceeding our hopes (Is. 49:19–21). To what extent this is true will be apparent to us in glory.

The Prayer — Pray today, praising God once again for redeeming you and everyone through His Servant, His Son and our Savior, Jesus.

The Insight — Store in your memory this passage: "God does not show favoritism but accepts men from every nation who fear him and do what is right" (Acts 10:34–35).

Week Eight

Monday

A PERSECUTOR PERISHES

The Light What does the information given to us in this chapter about Herod disclose about this ruler?

Read Acts 12.

Four generations of Herods appear in the New Testament. Most of them were ambitious, cynical, and murderous men. The first, *Herod the Great,* ruled from 47 to 4 B.C. Mentioned in Matt. 2 and Luke 1:5, he ruled Judea when Jesus was born. Herod the Great divided his kingdom among three sons. *Archelaus* received Judea, Samaria, and Idumaea and reigned from 4 B.C. to A.D. 6, when the Romans deposed him for maladministration and replaced him with a Roman official called a procurator. Archelaus is mentioned in Matt. 2:22. *Herod Antipas* ruled Galilee and Perea from 4 B.C. to A.D. 39. He is mentioned in Matt. 14; Mark 6 and 8; Luke 3, 9, 13, and 23; and Acts 4. Antipas executed John the Baptist and interrogated Jesus. *Philip* ruled Gaulantis, Iturea, and Trachonitis from 4 B.C. to A.D 34. He is mentioned at Luke 3:1. (The Philip referred to in Matt. 14 and Mark 6 is not the ruler Philip, but a half brother of Antipas. Philip the ruler, however, did later marry Salome, the daughter of Herodias referred to in Matt. 14:6–8 and Mark 6:22–28.) *Herod Agrippa I* is the Herod of Acts 12. He was the grandson of Herod the Great and the son of Aristobulus. In A.D. 37 he received the territory of his uncle Philip, in 40 the territory of his uncle Antipas, and in 41 Judea and Samaria (which his uncle Archelaus had inherited). He died in 44. The last Herod of the line was *Herod Agrippa II,* the son of Herod Agrippa I. He received Gaulantis, Ituraea, and Trachonitis in 53, and Judea and Samaria in 61. He died in Rome in about 100. He is the Agrippa of Acts 25 and 26. His sister Bernice was apparently his mistress (and the mistress of several others, as well, including the Roman emperor Titus).

The Way Though chosen by Herod Agrippa I as a convenient pawn in currying favor with his subjects, Peter was under the protection of a far greater power. Once again Ps. 2 applies, for the believers cited this psalm in Acts 4:23–30.

"**It must be** his angel," the assembled believers told Rhoda (Acts 12:15). The belief that each child of God has an assigned guardian angel seems supported here (as also in Matt. 18:10).

The Prayer Pray today, thanking God for watching over you.

The Insight No key can lock a door that God wants open.

THE SENDOFF

The Light What arguments does Paul use to convince the congregation at Antioch that Jesus is the Messiah?

Read Acts 13.

Paul's career as God's "chosen instrument to carry my name before the Gentiles and their kings and before the people of Israel" (9:15) finally takes off in this chapter. To this point we have followed Saul from his days as a zealous persecutor of the church to his remarkable conversion, through a stormy period as an apologist and evangelist in Damascus and Jerusalem to seclusion in Tarsus, and through service on the pastoral staff of the congregation at Antioch, Syria, which includes a charitable mission to bring aid to victims of drought in Judea. Now the Holy Spirit taps Barnabas and Saul (from now on, Paul) for the first of a series of missionary tours. The Holy Spirit calls the two through the congregation, which installs them in their office. Throughout his career Paul returns to Antioch as his base.

The Way The greater part of the account of the first missionary journey is devoted to Paul's address to the synagogue congregation at Antioch, Pisidia. Paul briefly reviews the history of Israel from the patriarchal period to David. He then identifies Jesus as the Messiah, the promised son of David. To prove this assertion Paul marshals three proofs. First, he turns to John the Baptist's testimony pointing to Jesus as the Savior. Then, recounting Jesus' crucifixion, he declares that Jesus' resurrection shows Him to be the Son of God. Finally, he quotes Scripture to show that Jesus fulfills the prophecies about the Messiah. He concludes with an admonition to heed Scripture's warning against rejecting God's Word. No doubt this account of Paul's remarks provides only a summary of his entire address.

Jealousy of Paul's success moves the synagogue leaders to reject the Gospel and to incite persecution against the missionaries. An unworthy motive prompts the leaders' unworthy response. Nevertheless, Paul and Barnabas leave a Spirit-filled church behind them at this Antioch, too. God's Word is never without effect.

The Prayer Pray today that the Gospel will continue to find a worthy response in your community.

The Insight We honor God's Word by believing it; we dishonor ourselves by rejecting it.

Week Eight

OPPOSITION ON TWO FRONTS

The Light **From the opposition** and misunderstanding Paul and Barnabas encountered, what can we learn about the world to which they brought the Gospel?

Read Acts 14.

The missionaries' itinerary took them first to *Salamis,* on the eastern shore of Cyprus, a city colonized by Phoenicians from Tyre centuries before. They crossed the island to *Paphos,* the seat of the Roman administration. They then sailed northwest 170 miles to the south central coast of Asia Minor, following the river Cestrus 12 miles inland to *Perga,* where Artemis (Diana), an Asiatic nature goddess, had a temple. (Paul was to confront the same cult in Ephesus— Acts 19:23–41.) They then journeyed northwest to *Antioch* of Pisidia, where many Jews had settled during the intertestamental period. Eighty miles southeast was *Iconium,* (still a populous Turkish city, Konya). Lystra lay 18 miles southwest, established as a Roman colony by Caesar Augustus in 6 B.C. At *Derbe,* 30 miles southeast, the missionaries turned and retraced their steps.

The Way **Two faiths** confront the messengers of the Gospel in these cities of Asia Minor. The first is *Judaism;* Jewish communities existed throughout the Mediterranean world at this time. Most major cities and towns contained at least one synagogue. Not only Jews and proselytes (circumcised Gentiles) but also some uncircumcised Gentiles (usually called "God-fearers") also worshiped each Sabbath. Although the missionaries usually won a nucleus for a Christian congregation by preaching in these synagogues, the Jews in them also usually produced a core of active opposition that stirred up enmity against the Gospel in their communities. Second, the missionaries encountered *pagan* temples where most local residents worshiped deities familiar to us through ancient Greek and classical literature. The mistaken identity of Paul and Barnabas as Hermes and Zeus probably resulted from a familiar legend, related by the Roman poet Ovid, in which these two gods appeared in human form to an aged couple, Philemon and Baucis.

In each new congregation Paul and Barnabas provided for continuation and growth by return visits, by writing letters, and by ordaining pastors, or elders (vv. 21–23). What a wonderful way God has provided for our Christian growth and support through our own congregations!

The Prayer **Pray today** for your congregation, that it may be a Gospel-centered base for growth and loving fellowship.

The Insight **The flight** to glory is seldom direct (v. 22).

53

COUNCIL IN A CRISIS

The Light **What issue** confronted the council at Jerusalem? How serious was this issue to the integrity of the church?

Read Acts 15.

Jewish Christianity separated from Judaism slowly—often only because Judaism expelled Christians as an intolerable sect. Christian Jews continued to frequent the temple so long as this was possible. Paul and other Christian evangelists attended services and preached in synagogues as long as they were permitted. Nevertheless, various issues produced lines of separation that divided Christians and unbelieving Jews. First, of course, was the acceptance of Jesus as the Messiah. Second was the necessity of observing the ceremonial law. Third was fellowship with ceremonially unclean Gentile believers, that is, Gentiles who were not circumcised and did not keep the ceremonial law. Some Jews became Christians while retaining their status as Pharisees (v. 5). They, and perhaps others, maintained that before Gentiles could become Christians they first must be circumcised and become obedient to the ceremonial law. Paul refers to this party as "the circumcision group" (Gal. 2:12). We often refer to them as Judaizers.

The Way **No mere difference** on indifferent matters was involved. The apostles recognized that the heart of Gospel Christianity was at stake in the dispute. Peter and Paul bring their own experience to bear on the issue, demonstrating that the Holy Spirit Himself directed and then vindicated the acceptance of the Gentiles on no other basis than faith in Christ. Then James decides the matter, citing the evidence of inspired Scripture—always the clinching argument in deciding matters of faith. Peter decisively states the crucial point when he declares, "We believe it is through the grace of our Lord Jesus that we are saved, just as they are" (v. 11).

A wise solution issues from the council. In deference to Jewish sensitivities, the council asked Gentile Christians to refrain from consuming blood and the meat of animals killed by strangulation (where the blood would remain within the carcass), from food sacrificed to idols, and from the immorality so prevalent within pagan society. We also need to be sensitive to the feelings of others, even when doing so means yielding rights. (See 1 Cor. 8.) The Jewish Christians, on the other hand, did not insist on other than these minimal requirements.

The Prayer **Pray today** that God might help resolve disagreements on the basis of sound Scriptural principles.

The Insight **Truth and love** are the right tools to resolve disputes.

NEW RECRUITS

The Light What important transition does the statement in verse 5 signal?

Read Acts 16.

Paul's colleagues have consisted of *Barnabas* and *Mark*. A "sharp disagreement" (15:39) results in Paul and Barnabas going separate ways, Barnabas (with his cousin Mark) to his native Cyprus (4:36), and Paul and *Silas* going overland from Antioch to visit previously established churches at Derbe, Lystra, Iconium, and Antioch of Pisidia. We first meet Silas (or Silvanus) at 15:22, where Silas is one of two envoys from the apostolic council at Jerusalem to the Gentile believers at Antioch of Syria. Silas accompanied Paul as far as Corinth; after that he is no longer mentioned. (Peter, however, refers to Silas as assisting him in writing to the churches in Asia Minor.)

The Way Two new companions join Paul in this chapter. *Timothy*, introduced in verse one, becomes Paul's "true son in the faith" (1 Tim. 1:2), to whom the elder apostle addresses two inspired epistles when the young Timothy served the important congregation at Ephesus. Traditional sources tell us that Timothy died a martyr there and was succeeded by the apostle John. Besides Acts and Hebrews, 10 of Paul's 13 epistles refer to Timothy—a testimony to Timothy's importance to Paul. The other companion of Paul introduced in this chapter is unnamed.

We become aware of his presence with Paul only indirectly by a self-effacing "we." This modest companion is undoubtedly *Luke*, who joined Paul at Troas (16:10) and went with him to Philippi, where we lose sight of him (at 16:17) until Paul leaves Philippi (20:5) and goes to Miletus (20:15), a port near Ephesus. Luke accompanies Paul to Jerusalem (21:1–18) and joins Paul when he is in custody on his way to Rome to stand trial (27:1–28:16). Paul sends greetings from Luke to Colossae (Col. 4: 14), written while Paul was awaiting trial in Rome and expecting to be released soon (Philemon 22). Luke also stood by Paul during his second imprisonment (2 Tim. 4:11), when Paul believed himself to be near the end of his apostolic career (vv. 6–8).

An important transition is signaled by the summary statement at 16:5. (For other such statements see 6:7; 9:31; 12:24; 19:20; and 28:31.) By the Lord's own direction Paul is to take the Gospel to Macedonia, a giant step forward to "the ends of the earth" (1:8). What opportunities is the Lord giving you to share the Gospel with others?

The Prayer Pray today by name for your Christian friends and partners in the Gospel that the Lord might bless your joint work and fellowship.

The Insight He, we; the Lord, the church.

Week Eight

MOSES' SUCCESSOR

The Light — Why was Joshua selected as the successor of Moses?

Read Numbers 13–14, 27:12–23.

Paul the apostle seems to hold the record among major Bible figures in terms of the number of their co-workers. Paging through Acts and Paul's epistles, we can identify at least 14 persons whom Paul identifies as working closely with him—and this does not include any of the Twelve, who also might be considered Paul's colleagues in ministry. But Paul is hardly alone in carrying on a collegial ministry. Closely associated with Peter was Mark, and Peter also acknowledges the assistance of Silas. In the Old Testament, also, we find partners in ministry. Jeremiah had Baruch, Elijah had Elisha, and Moses had Aaron (and Eleazar his successor), Miriam, and Joshua. Joshua served as Moses' aide at Sinai (Ex. 24:13). Later, Joshua appears as a leader of the tribe of Ephraim and is its representative on the party sent to scout out the land God had promised. When the time came to select a successor for Moses, God himself chose Joshua and ordered his commissioning by having Moses lay his hands on his successor in the presence of the high priest (an act at which the Spirit that guided Moses passed to Moses' successor—Deut. 34:9).

The Way — Joshua possessed many fine qualities that made him the right man to lead Israel. He had gained experience as Moses' aide. He displayed courage. But his most important qualification was a faith that caused him to trust and obey the Lord with a consistency we do not see even in Moses himself. The argument of Joshua and Caleb for entering the land was simple and direct: "If the Lord is pleased with us, he will lead us into that land. . . . Only do not rebel against the LORD. . . . The LORD is with us" (14:8–9).

"A man in whom is the Spirit"—that was Joshua's strength. Is the Holy Spirit of God also your strength?

The Prayer — Pray today for the Spirit-given courage to do the Lord's will in everything, no matter how great the obstacles.

The Insight — Store in your memory this passage: "Believe in the Lord Jesus, and you will be saved" (Acts 16:31).

RESPONSES

The Light What responses to the Gospel do you find in this chapter?

Read Acts 17.

As usual, Paul proclaimed the Gospel at Thessalonica and at Berea first in Jewish synagogues, showing by the Old Testament Scriptures that Jesus is the Messiah. And as usual, Paul's preaching drew varying responses. Some Jews bitterly opposed the Gospel. But some believed. Even more receptive were the "God-fearing Greeks and not a few prominent women" (v. 4). These Gentiles had perceived the great difference between pagan religions and superstitions and the faith of Israel in the sovereign Lord of heaven and earth. No doubt Jewish neighbors had shared this faith with them. That there were "God-fearers" throughout the Mediterranean world is a tribute to the Jewish communities scattered about this area. Now these believing Gentiles were ready to receive the Messiah they had learned about in the Old Testament writings. In this respect these Gentiles were like the "more noble" Berean Jews who were ready to accept Jesus as the Messiah when they found from the Scriptures that "what Paul said was true" (v. 11).

The Way A different audience awaited Paul in Athens, a great intellectual center of its day. The two most prominent schools of philosophy were the Stoics (who advocated a more austere approach to life) and the Epicureans (who thought that indulging the sensual appetites could not harm the integrity of philosophic pursuits). Although ready to consider new ideas, these intellectuals were less than ready to accept them. They particularly resisted Paul's reference to Jesus' resurrection since it contradicts the conclusions of both human experience and reason. (See 1 Cor. 1:20–25.)

A few Athenians believed the Gospel, though most either openly sneered or politely put if off (v. 32). But God's Word will not be put off.

The Prayer Pray today that those who hear the Gospel from you and your congregation may believe it.

The Insight The final stage of the Gospel's journey to the heart is the most difficult.

FELLOW WORKERS

The Light

Note the names of those who serve with or assist Paul as you read.

Read Acts 18.

Others who assisted Paul in some way are introduced to us in this chapter. Three of them become Paul's colleagues in the Christian mission. *Aquila* and *Priscilla* were the only couple whom the New Testament describes as engaged in evangelism. They are always mentioned together. We cannot tell whether they became Christians in Rome or were converted by Paul in Corinth. They shared a common trade with Paul, who lived and worked with them in Corinth. They accompanied Paul to Ephesus, where they evidently remained for some time, since they were still there when Paul wrote to the Corinthian congregation during his third missionary journey (1 Cor. 16:19). They later returned to Rome; Paul greets and warmly praises them in his letter to Rome (Rom. 16:3). *Apollos* a Jew from Alexandria, Egypt, is already a Christian when he arrives in Ephesus. He is, nevertheless, deficient in Christian doctrine, a deficiency that Aquila and Priscilla corrected. Apollos then went to Corinth, where he became a popular leader of the local congregation (1 Cor. 1:12; 3:5, 22; 4:6), and later

returned to Asia (16:12). *Tiberius Justus* was a Gentile "God-fearer" who opened his home as a Christian gathering place. *Crispus,* the synagogue ruler who accepted the Gospel, is mentioned by Paul (in 1 Cor. 1:14) as one of those few whom he personally baptized. *Sosthenes,* the synagogue ruler who persecuted the church and was beaten for his efforts, may later have become a Christian himself (1 Cor. 1:1).

The Way

"I have many people in this city," the Lord told Paul in Corinth. And a mighty (if troubled) church did grow there. Already before they heard and believed the Gospel, the Lord knew who would be His. In this connection see Rom. 8:29–30 and John 10:16.

"I will come back if it is God's will," Paul said to the Christians of Ephesus. He had completely turned himself and his plans over to the Lord's will. Have we?

The Prayer

Pray today for Christians whose knowledge of Christian doctrine is incomplete or mistaken, that God might correct and perfect them for His service.

The Insight

We all need God above us and others beside us.

Week Nine

Wednesday

PAUL IN EPHESUS

The Light How do the events recorded in this chapter testify to Paul's great success in Ephesus?

Read Acts 19.

Paul had visited Ephesus briefly on his second missionary journey (18:19–21). But his major influence there came on his third journey, when he devoted two years of ministry to this important city, the capitol of the Roman province of Asia. In apostolic times Ephesus was one of three great cities of the eastern Mediterranean. (The others were Antioch in Syria and Alexandria in Egypt.) Major highways and sea-lanes converged at Ephesus. But the city's greatest claim to distinction was that it was "the guardian of the temple of the great Artemis and of her image, which fell from heaven" (v. 35). The temple of Artemis (or Diana) at Ephesus was regarded as one of the seven wonders of the ancient world and may well have been the largest building in existence when Paul resided in the city. The image may have been a meteorite resembling the many-breasted female figure of the goddess of fertility. Artemis was worshiped also in other places, but Ephesus held a primacy in her cult.

The Way Paul's success in preaching the Gospel in Ephesus receives reverse tribute in the fear that "the goddess herself, who is worshiped throughout the province of Asia and the world, will be robbed of her divine majesty" (v. 27). Though probably deliberately overstated, this prediction did come true, as Ephesus later became a great Christian center where an important ecumenical council took place in 431. Paul's success also affected the Jewish community of Ephesus, causing "the name of the Lord Jesus" to be "held in high honor" by believers and unbelievers alike. Contributing to this reputation was the embarrassing incident involving the sons of a chief priest, Sceva (a Latinized name—his Jewish name might have enabled us to recognize this priest), who were functioning as exorcists. (See Luke 11:19.) Many magicians and astrologers, a common occupation in those highly superstitious times, also converted to Christ and burned their books.

Baptism into Christ as Savior is a necessary part of becoming a Christian. Baptism applies the accomplishments of Christ's sacrifice and resurrection to us so that we are saved. (See Rom. 6:1–10 and 1 Peter 3:21.) Thank God for your Christian baptism.

The Prayer Pray today, praising God that the Gospel wins human hearts (including your own) and saves them from false belief, unbelief, and superstition.

The Insight Enemy opposition pays tribute to the Gospel.

Week Nine

Thursday

A FOND FAREWELL

The Light What instructions does Paul give the elders (pastors) of the congregation at Ephesus?

Read Acts 20.

Homeward bound to Jerusalem to keep a date with the Lord that will take him to Rome, Paul delivers farewell addresses to the church at Troas and (at Miletus) to the elders of Ephesus. His farewell at Troas, delivered in an upstairs meeting hall, lasted into the night. The late hour and the warm, heavy air from the burning lamps causes an unhappy accident for one young listener but also an opportunity for Paul to display the mercy and the power of Christ. The service then continues and includes the breaking of bread. Luke uses the same words in Acts 2:42, and Paul uses them in 1 Cor. 10 and 11. Paul obviously means Holy Communion when he speaks of breaking bread. Does Luke? The context would allow that meaning but certainly does not require it. Eating together was an expression of fellowship in the early church, as it is for us, but early Christians included the Lord's Supper in the occasion, which was called a "love feast."

The Way Paul calls the elders of Ephesus to him at Miletus. He wishes to give the church important parting instructions, but he could not take the time to visit the congregation itself (v. 16). He has an urgent warning for this congregation where he had spent more time than with any other. He forsees the coming of false teachers who will "draw away disciples" from the Gospel to their own distortions of the truth. He refers to the congregation as a flock of sheep, to the elders as shepherds (the Latin word for shepherd is pastor), and to the false teachers as wolves—a metaphor also used by the Old Testament prophets (for example, Ezek. 34), by Jesus (Matt. 7:15; 10:16; John 10:1–18), and by other apostles (1 Peter 2:25; 5:2–4).

Paul set an example of working hard to help the weak (vv. 35–36). Do we set the same example?

The Prayer Pray today for your pastor, that he may faithfully fulfill his work as a shepherd over God's flock, won by Christ's blood.

The Insight Farewells are easier when we all keep in touch with the Lord.

Week Nine

Friday

UNDER ARREST

The Light What charges against Paul caused the riot resulting in his arrest?

Read Acts 21.

The same persecutors who opposed Paul in Antioch of Pisidia (13:45, 50), Iconium (14:2, 4–5), Lystra (14:19), Thessalonica (17:5–9), and Berea (17:13) nip at Paul's heels also in Jerusalem. They use the same method as before, making up outrageous charges to incite mobs against him. Specifically in Jerusalem, they accuse Paul of teaching "all men everywhere against our people and our law and this place" and of defiling the temple by bringing Gentiles into it. Gentiles could enter the outer area (the Court of the Gentiles) but could go no farther, under penalty of death. They made this latter charge on an assumption. As Paul's willingness to undergo Jewish purification rites and to support those who were fulfilling vows shows (vv. 23–24, 26—see also 16:3; 18:18), he was no radical iconoclast. He had abided by the letter and the spirit of the decree of the Jerusalem Council (15:28–29; 16:4), which asked Gentiles to respect Jewish customs while not requiring Gentiles to become Jews before they could become Christian. For Paul's rule in this matter, see 1 Cor. 7:17–20 and 9:19–23.

The Way As for Jewish Christians in Judea, the report given to Paul by the apostles and elders would suggest that they continued to practice circumcision and to observe Jewish customs and traditions (vv. 20–21—see also 15:5). Some of these Jewish Christians failed to appreciate the fact that Christ has freed us from the Law by fulfilling it on our behalf (Gal. 3:13–14, 23–25), but we should not assume that this was true of all Jewish Christians who continued to observe the law but in a spirit of faith.

Though forewarned that he would have trouble (20:22–24; 21:10–14), Paul determined to keep the path the Lord marked out for him, trusting God for strength. What an example for us!

The Prayer Pray today for faithfulness, courage, and strength to be Christ's person where you are.

The Insight Though the devil's arms are long, God's are longer and stronger.

GOD GOVERNS

The Light Why did Joseph's brothers sell him to slave traders?

Read Genesis 37 and 45.

Living with a superior person who knows and speaks frankly of his superiority is not easy. It requires a level of humility and self-esteem most of us do not possess. Neither did Joseph's brothers have such qualities. Joseph was born to greatness, and God revealed this to him early in life. Joseph relates with naiveté (not boastfulness) dreams in which God disclosed his future greatness. But his brothers become so jealous and resentful that all but Reuben plot his murder and, failing that, sell their brother into slavery. They then cruelly deceive their father, telling the old man that his favorite son was dead. Surely we can find little to justify such hatred and resentment. "You intended to harm me," Joseph told his brothers later, "but God intended it for good to accomplish what is now being done, the saving of many lives" (Gen. 50:20).

The Way God governs events, even those brought about by evil motives, so that they serve His kingdom. "God sent me ahead of you to preserve for you a remnant on earth and to save your lives by a great deliverance" (45:7). God intended to bless all humanity through Abraham's Seed, and so he preserved Israel, using the hateful motives of Joseph's brothers in the service of His purpose. God used the sinister efforts of those who opposed the Gospel to send Paul on to Rome so that Paul might proclaim the Gospel there. But the supreme example of God's use of the motives of dishonorable people to achieve His saving purpose occurred when He let them seize and crucify His own Son. Their designs were evil, but God's plan was good.

Forgiveness and desire for reconciliation filled Joseph's heart when he recognized his brothers before him. May God remove all bitterness and desire for vengeance from us and fill us with Joseph's spirit.

The Prayer Pray today for someone who has suffered wrong, that God might enable that person to forgive.

The Insight Store in your memory this passage: "Keep watch over yourselves and all the flock of which the Holy Spirit has made you overseers. Be shepherds of the church of God, which he bought with his own blood" (Acts 20:28).

Week Ten

CHRIST'S WITNESS

The Light What explanation does Paul offer for his Gospel ministry among the Gentiles?

Read Acts 22.

A straightforward account of how he came to be a missionary sent by Jesus to the Gentiles constitutes Paul's defense. His address emphasizes his common ground with those who accuse him. He addresses them in their native tongue as "brothers and fathers." He identifies himself as a Jew, brought up in Jerusalem, instructed by a revered Jewish sage. He calls on the high priest to testify to his zeal as a persecutor of Christians. He relates that he was on his way to do more such work when Jesus stopped him and sent Ananias (whose upright character as a devout observer of the Law is attested) to baptize him. Paul recalls that later, in a vision in the temple at Jerusalem, Jesus spoke to him again and commissioned him as an apostle to the Gentiles. Paul simply tells what happened to him. He stands where he does not by his own design or plan but because God put him there. Paul is serving as a witness; he tells what he has seen and heard.

The Way In doing so, Paul provides a model for our own witnessing. When we teach or communicate God's Word, we pass that Word along faithfully, not adding our own opinions to it. But when we serve as witnesses, we tell truthfully how the Lord has acted in our lives. We tell what God has done for us. Matthias was qualified to be added to the apostles because he had observed the Lord, heard Him, and had seen Him after the resurrection (Acts 1:21–26). Peter declared, "We are witnesses of" Jesus' crucifixion and resurrection (3:15). Peter and John told the Sanhedrin, "We cannot help speaking about what we have seen and heard" (4:20).

Paul claimed his privileges as a Roman citizen. But he also enjoyed far greater privileges as a citizen of God's kingdom. So do we. (See Phil. 3:20; Eph. 2:19–20; and 1 Peter 2:9–10.)

The Prayer Pray today, asking God to make you a bolder and more effective witness of His grace to you.

The Insight Christ opens our hearts to love, opens our hands to give, opens our mouths to witness.

GOD'S MAN BEFORE
THE WORLD'S COURTS

The Light Evaluate the competency of the officials before whom Paul appears as you read.

Read Acts 23.

Religious and civil officials who presided over Judea in apostolic times were notoriously corrupt. The cruelty and immorality of *the Herodian rulers* were so great that these cynical despots murdered family and friends as well as foes when they believed it served their own best interest. All too often, the procurators, *the Roman officials* who ruled Judea, proved to be incompetent, insensitive, or dishonest—or all three. Even *the Jewish high priesthood* was passed about as a political plum. Though supposedly chosen for life, high priests were often removed after a short time in office because political powers, both Jewish and Roman, had shifted. The whole shoddy array appears in the gospels and in Acts. Paul correctly labels Ananias a "whitewashed wall," whose hypocritical facade hardly covered the reality of his lawlessness. This man, who occupied Judaism's holiest office, was ready to enter into a plot to ambush and murder a man who could not be convicted legally. Paul exposes the incompetence of Israel's highest religious court by a mere reference to a doctrine that divided its members.

The Way Though facing such unscrupulous and dangerous opponents, Paul trusted himself to the Lord. The world's rulers are as nothing in God's hand. He uses them to accomplish His holy will. The Lord intended to bring Paul to Rome, the seat of the world's power in that day, so that he might serve there as God's witness. Though God's opponents may posture and parade their supposed power, God regards them as puny and ridiculous. (See Ps. 2.)

We also may be confident of God's power to preserve his Word and church. We may serve His will with assurance, knowing that His kingdom will come and His will will be done, no matter what or who may oppose Him.

The Prayer Pray today for the courage to trust God to protect you as you serve Him.

The Insight God has His eye on those who cry.

TRUE AND FALSE

The Light

What defense does Paul offer regarding the charges against him?

Read Acts 24.

Like Jesus before Pontius Pilate, Paul stood before a Roman procurator, Felix. Considerable hypocrisy was evident in Felix's detainment of Paul. The high priest and his fellow complainants knowingly filed charges that were not based on fact. The lawyer, in praising Felix (vv. 2–4), was being hypocritical; the Jews hated Felix and sent a delegation to Rome to bring charges against him. Finally, Felix himself was hypocritical. In granting Paul an audience before him and his wife Drusilla, Felix wished to give Paul an opportunity to offer a bribe. Since no bribe was forthcoming, Felix left Paul in prison, hoping to gain at least something from the Jews. Leadership was deteriorating rapidly in Judea during this period; public order would soon disappear altogether, until Judea revolted against Rome in A.D. 66. Roman forces under Titus would put down the revolt at a terrible cost to the Jews, including the destruction of Jerusalem in A.D. 70.

The Way

Two charges against Paul were laid before Felix. First, Paul was named a troublemaker and "a ringleader of the Nazarene sect." Second, he was charged with trying "to desecrate the temple" (vv. 5–6). Paul answers the second charge first, denying that he had desecrated the temple in any way. To the first charge, he admitted to being "a follower of the Way, which they call a sect" (v. 14). But as to stirring up riots, he did nothing of the sort. His opponents were the real agitators, deliberately setting off riots by planting outrageous rumors.

Paul gladly acknowledged being a Christian, even in a hostile setting. Are we ready to acknowledge our faith before others?

The Prayer

Pray today for Christians under trial for their faith, that God might grant them courage and trust in God.

The Insight

Christ's name to claim—not our shame but our fame!

PAUL'S APPEAL

The Light

Why did Paul appeal his case to Caesar?

Read Acts 25.

Paul merited the special treatment he received—personal hearings before two Roman procurators and then before Caesar himself—because he was a Roman citizen. Rome ruled the Mediterranean world (including northern and western Europe as far as Britain, eastern Europe as far as Russia, the eastern Mediterranean area as far as the Caspian Sea, and north Africa from Egypt to present-day Morocco). Thus, those with full Roman citizenship within this mighty empire enjoyed worthwhile privilege. Being a citizen of Rome carried with it rights and privileges unavailable to other people who were mere residents of subjugated lands. At first, as the term implies, Roman citizenship came with being born in Rome or within the territory immediately adjacent to it. But as the empire expanded, citizenship was given to others as a reward. Foreign soldiers who served in Rome's military forces might be granted citizenship on retirement as a reward for faithful service. Occasionally whole cities might be granted Roman citizenship. The privilege was usually extended to descendants as well. Since Paul, a Jew, was "born a citizen" (Acts 22:28), his father or grandfather must have been granted citizenship for some reason.

The Way

Paul exercised his rights and privileges to protect himself in the service of the Gospel. Christians should not seek persecution or suffering for the cause of Christ nor should they deny the Lord or His Word to avoid it. The Lord intended to bring Paul to Rome so that the apostle might serve as His witness there (Acts 23:11). The Lord used Paul's rights as a Roman citizen to bring about that end.

Paul's only offense was that he claimed and proclaimed Christ in a world hostile to the Lord. May that be our only offense, an offense of which we may stand convicted.

The Prayer

Pray today for the wisdom and willingness to place our status in this world at the Lord's service.

The Insight

All Christians are well born.

FACING DOWN THE FAMOUS

The Light — What effect does Paul's defense have on Festus and Agrippa?

Read Acts 26.

"You will be brought before kings and governors, and all on account of my name. This will result in your being witnesses to them. But make up your mind not to worry beforehand how you will defend yourselves. For I will give you words and wisdom that none of your adversaries will be able to resist or contradict" (Luke 21:12–15). This prediction of Jesus is fulfilled in Paul, who has offered his defense before one governor, Felix, and who now presents the same defense to another, Festus; to a king, Herod Agrippa II; and before "the leading men of the city" (Caesarea). Paul's witness is powerful, unnerving even these powerful people. "As Paul discoursed on righteousness, self-control, and the judgment to come, Felix was afraid and said, 'That's enough for now!' " (24:25). Festus is moved to shout, "You are out of your mind, Paul! . . . Your great learning is driving you insane" (26:24). But it is Festus's mind, not Paul's, that is disturbed. Paul has stated, "I am saying nothing beyond what the prophets and Moses said would happen—that the Christ would suffer and, as the first to rise from the dead, would proclaim light to his own people and to the Gentiles" (vv. 22–23). He follows up, turning to the king, "King Agrippa, do you believe the prophets? I know you do." To which the king can but stammer, "Do you think that in such a short time you can persuade me to be a Christian?" (vv. 27–28). Both rulers then retreat.

The Way — Paul's boldness comes from another King—the King of kings (Rev. 19:16). Of this greater King, Paul is an "ambassador in chains" (Eph. 6:20). But Paul is not that King's only ambassador; we also are "Christ's ambassadors," and we also offer a gracious, royal invitation, as Paul did in verse 29: "Be reconciled to God" (2 Cor. 5:20).

Paul pointed to Christ as being altogether responsible for his own dramatic turnaround. Paul acted on the confidence that the Christ who could convert a zealous persecutor could also convert a Gentile governor or a corrupt king. Do we share that confidence—that anyone is within the Spirit's grasp? Do we act on it?

The Prayer — Pray today for the courage needed to testify before kings— that you might speak of Jesus to a friend, a relative, or a neighbor.

The Insight — Standing up for Jesus can happen when He puts us on our feet.

Week Ten

Saturday

A PROPHET'S REBUKE

The Light **Evaluate** the characters of Ahab and Jezebel as they are presented to us in this chapter.

Read 1 Kings 21.

Three dramatic figures appear before us on the stage of this chapter. The royal pair, King Ahab and Queen Jezebel, are surely among the most prominent of Scripture's villains. As for Ahab, he "did more evil in the eyes of the Lord than any of those before him" (1 Kings 16:30), engaging in idolatry on a scale that made previous idolatries "trivial" (16:31). Ahab flagrantly disobeyed God both by committing idolatry and by contracting forbidden political alliances (16:29–34; 20:31–34). Yet Ahab was a weak person, completely dominated by his even more evil wife, Jezebel. A princess of Sidon (16:31), this thoroughly malicious woman brought her worship of false deities with her. Apparently without any scruples or conscience, she could commit perjury, murder, and theft without a moment's hesitation. Whereas Ahab could be moved to repentance, Jezebel remained defiant until her horrible death (2 Kings 9:30–37).

The Way **To confront** this evil pair with the Lord's judgment against their crimes, God sent one of Israel's most dramatic figures, Elijah. So powerful is this spokesman of the Lord that he is chosen as the prototype of John the Baptist, called to prepare Israel for the Messiah's coming (Luke 1:76; 9:8; Matt. 11:14). Elijah represents all the prophets, and Moses the Law, as they confer with Jesus when the Savior is transfigured (Luke 9:30). Alone among Israel's prophets, Elijah does not die but is taken directly to heaven (2 Kings 2:11). Such a man could confront a king as greater than an equal, as the Lord's own mouth. Yet even this extraordinary man is a mere man, in need of God's gentle rebuke, forgiveness, encouragement, and strengthening. He dared to take on a king, as did Nathan (2 Sam. 12) and Paul (Acts 24–26), by the command and strength of the Lord.

"So you have found me, my enemy!" (1 Kings 21:20). How terrible to have to regard the Lord and his spokesman as an enemy! Yet apart from God's grace in Christ, we are all His enemies (Col. 1:21). But in Christ we have become His friends (John 15:14–15).

The Prayer **Pray today** for someone you know, or know about, who is at war with God, that this person might be reconciled through faith in Christ.

The Insight **Store in your memory** this passage: "Why should any of you consider it incredible that God raises the dead?" (Acts 26:8).

Week Eleven

A TERRIFYING TRIP

The Light **What permitted Paul** to remain calm and confident on this terrifying voyage?

Read Acts 27.

The world in which the apostles lived ringed the Mediterranean Sea. Paul was never more than 300 miles from its shores and hardly ever more than 100 miles away. Ships, naturally enough, were common modes of transport and travel from one side of the sea to another. Yet sea travel was often dangerous. Winter on the Mediterranean was apt to be stormy, creating a precarious situation for crew and passengers caught in a wooden boat on the open sea. Merchant ships carrying grain or other products such as wine, oil, and foods from north Africa to Rome were often 100 feet or more in length and could weigh 30 tons or better. Though such ships were primarily freight carriers, they often took on passengers as well. (Passenger ships, as such, however, seem to be unknown in apostolic times.) Though some ships included cabin accommodations, these would be reserved for the wealthy or prominent; most passengers had to be content with quarters in the hold or places on deck. With cargo on board, ships might carry from 200 to 600 people, including the crew. (The ship on which Paul was shipwrecked carried 276 passengers and crew.)

The Way **Being caught** in a storm at sea under such conditions would have been a terrifying experience. But Paul remained serene and calm, for the Lord had assured him that all aboard would survive for the sake of Paul's mission to Rome. How often the Lord preserves unbelievers for the sake of the church and its mission! Paul believed the Lord's assurance and was confident that his life and safety were in the trustworthy keeping of God.

Paul's confidence and faith encouraged the crew and other passengers. The example of our faith also may encourage and inspire others. Some may even come to share faith when they see how belief is backed up by conduct.

The Prayer **Pray today** for missionaries and other Christians whose discipleship puts them in danger, that God might protect and encourage them.

The Insight **Courage** accompanies Christian conviction.

Week Eleven

ARRIVAL IN ROME

The Light For what reason did Paul summon the Jewish leaders when he arrived in Rome?

Read Acts 28.

Though a prisoner, Paul enjoys considerable freedom. At Sidon, the officer in charge permits Paul "to go to his friends so they might provide for his needs" (27:3). His military escort, Justus, is kind to Paul, who is accorded an authoritative role on board ship. On Malta, after the shipwreck, the local governor, Publius, entertains Paul and Luke in his own home. Paul's healing of Publius's father and of "the rest of the sick on the island" (28:9) wins for the apostle the goodwill and the help of the islanders. On the last leg of his journey Paul is permitted to linger an entire week with Christians who came to meet him. And in Rome Paul "was allowed to live by himself," though chained to a soldier (28:16, 30–31). Why did Paul enjoy such liberties? We might think of several explanations. He was a Roman citizen and enjoyed certain rights (22:25–29; 25:16). Paul had not been convicted but was only going to stand trial. After pretrial hearings a Roman governor and a Jewish king expressed convictions of his innocence (26:31–32). Paul was going before the emperor by his own appeal (25:10–12, 21; 28:19). The two Roman officials, Justus the centurion and Publius the governor, liked Paul; it may even be that Luke's inclusion of their names suggests their later conversion to faith in Christ.

The Way God had brought Paul to Rome not for the convenience of Roman justice because of the Lord's plan for Paul's apostolic work. Paul wrote his letter to the Romans before his arrival there under guard, probably from Corinth toward the close of his third missionary journey. He expected to be released and to go on to Spain (Rom. 15:23–24). Perhaps he also visited churches in Asia Minor once more. Later he was arrested again, imprisoned, and executed (2 Tim. 4:6–8).

As usual, Paul first proclaimed the Gospel to the Jews (vv. 23–24), following the principle he expresses in Rom. 1:16. Some believed, but some rejected the Gospel. This did not surprise Paul (though it saddened him; see Rom. 9:1–3); the apostle found their behavior predicted already by the prophet Isaiah. As usual, Paul would take the next step, proclaiming the Gospel to the Gentiles. God's kingdom will come, if not with us, then without us.

The Prayer Pray today for freedom, both from external obstructions and internal reluctance, that will permit you and your church to proclaim God's Gospel.

The Insight Though the world's foot is on the accelerator, God's hand is on the wheel.

GALATIANS

Perhaps no other letter in the New Testament is as passionate as Paul's letter to the Galatians. Though written to people he knew personally, he makes no personal references. The letter breathes the air of crisis. After a brief preliminary greeting, Paul at once—almost abruptly—expresses the concern that caused him to write. He stays on the subject with a single-minded, passionate determination that will not let go until he has accomplished his aim.

Luke has introduced us to this crisis in the Book of Acts: "Some men came down from Judea to Antioch and were teaching the brothers: 'Unless you are circumcised, according to the custom taught by Moses, you cannot be saved'" (Acts 15:1). These of "the circumcision group" (Gal. 2:12) were Jews who taught a version of the Gospel that was actually a deadly perversion. They maintained that faith in Christ was not enough; obedience to the Law in every respect was also required for salvation. Paul saw that such an approach denied the Gospel and nullified the redemptive work of Christ.

Because of its passionate defense of salvation by grace through faith alone, the letter to the Galatians was a favorite epistle of Martin Luther, the 16th-century reformer of the church, who also contended for the truth that we are saved by grace alone, through faith alone, as taught by Scripture alone.

DEFENDER OF THE FAITH

The Light For what reason does Paul defend his status as an apostle?

Read Galatians 1.

Several features distinguish this letter from most of Paul's other letters. After the customary greeting (vv. 1–5), he immediately launches into the subject of his letter. There is no initial thanksgiving so typical of Paul's other letters. (For examples, see Rom. 1:8–10; 1 Cor. 1:4–9; 2 Cor. 1:3–7; and other letters.) Galatians is a single-subject letter that sustains a tone of urgency throughout. Only in the first half of the last chapter does Paul broaden his approach, but then he returns to the main subject as he concludes this sharply pointed admonition. Finally, the letter closes as abruptly as it began. There are no closing greetings— no references to individuals at all—either at the beginning of the letter or at the end. This is not Paul's usual gregarious approach. Look at the beginnings and closings of his other letters and see the difference.

The Way These features underline the urgency of this letter. Paul must immediately address a challenge that threatens to undermine the evangelistic work begun on his first missionary journey at Antioch, Iconium, Lystra, and Derbe (in an area then known as Lower Galatia). Teachers claiming to represent a more authentic, authoritative Christianity than what had been learned from Paul have come to Galatia. They presume to supplement and complete Paul's work. They charge that Paul has left out essential elements of Christian doctrine, such as the necessity of circumcision, obedience to the Law of Moses, and observance of dietary regulations. In making these charges, they cast doubt on Paul's authority and on the authenticity of his apostleship. He lacks proper credentials and (supposedly) the authorization of the real apostles, the Twelve.

Paul must defend his Gospel and apostolate, for it is not his but Christ's. That is precisely why we today also must speak up for and defend our Gospel and ministry, for it is Christ's. We may suffer the slander of our persons or reputations, but we must never permit the Lord's Gospel to suffer slander while we can defend it.

The Prayer Pray today for those called to defend Christian truth, that they may do it effectively and with love.

The Insight Christ defends His church by His Word; Christ defends His Word by His church.

Week Eleven

Thursday

SCOLDING AN APOSTLE

The Light Look for indications of how Paul views leadership in the church as you read.

Read Galatians 2.

Four times, accounts of Paul's conversion and of later events appear (in Acts 9:1–30; 22:2–21; 26:4–20; and here in Gal. 1:11–2:10—another note about Paul's activities between his conversion and the beginning of the first missionary journey occurs in Acts 11:25–30). Still, scholars cannot piece together a perfect chronology of his comings and goings between his conversion and first missionary tour because they cannot date the events with certainty. For example, is the visit to Jerusalem described in Gal. 2:1–10 the visit of Acts 11:25–30 or that of Acts 15:1–30? Or is it another visit altogether? Perhaps it is the latter. In Acts 11 and 15 the Antioch church sends Paul and Barnabas to Jerusalem, but here in Gal. 2 Paul goes "in response to a revelation." In Galatians, Paul and Barnabas take Titus, who is not mentioned in Acts 11 or 15. Furthermore, in Galatians Paul meets privately with the leaders in Jerusalem; in Acts 15 the meeting includes many people. The meeting in Galatians appears to be different from the events described in either Acts 11 or 15 and seems to have occurred sometime between them.

The Way Paul's view of leadership in the church is clear from his interaction with the church leaders in Jerusalem. On the one hand, he respects these leaders and regards their opinion as important (v. 2). That the Jerusalem leaders gave Paul and Barnabas "the right hand of fellowship" affirmed the validity of Paul's apostolic authority and vindicated him against the claims of opponents. Nevertheless, Paul will hold these leaders, too, under the far superior authority of God's revealed Word. He will not elevate them unduly; they *"seemed* to be leaders"* (v. 2); they *"seemed* to be important"* (v. 6). They were *"reputed* to be pillars"* (v. 9). "Whatever they were makes no difference to me; God does not judge by external appearance—those men added nothing to my message" (v. 6).

And Paul did not hesitate to scold Peter sharply when that apostle's behavior contradicted the Gospel and threatened to diminish the power of its liberating, gracious message. There are times when a rebuke is needed, perhaps even of a leader.

The Prayer Pray today for leaders in the church, that God might keep them humble and subject to His Word.

The Insight Love sometimes speaks with a sharp tongue.

LAW AND GOSPEL

The Light What are the distinctive roles of Law and Gospel in the life of a Christian?

Read Galatians 3.

Two distinct principles appear throughout the Bible. These principles do not contradict one another but work in tension with each other. We usually refer to the principles as Law and Gospel. The Law discloses our obligations to God (v. 12), and it curses the one who fails to fulfill these obligations (v. 10). The Gospel reveals the grace of God that reached its fulfillment in Jesus Christ. Both are the Word of God, and as such, both are holy. But which principle takes precedence over the other? Paul answers that question in his letter to the Galatians. His opponents (he calls them the "circumcision group," 2:12) insisted, in effect, that the Law takes precedence over the Gospel. They saw the Gospel as having an intermediate role, as providing a needed boost for the sinner, enabling a child of God to obey the Law. Alert Christians recognize that this view still plagues the church today.

The Way Paul defends the precedence of the Gospel. First, the Gospel has *historical precedence* (vv. 8, 17). Immediately after the Fall God announced His plan to send the Savior (Gen. 3:15). When the Lord called Abram, He restated that plan and began to set it in motion. At that time He declared that "all peoples on earth will be blessed through you." God established His covenant with Abraham and with his progeny on that promise. The covenant based on the Law did not come until the time of Moses, nearly 500 years later. Second, the Gospel takes *precedence in its purpose.* The Law is to serve the purpose of the Gospel, not the other way around (vv. 19, 22–25). The Law convicts us of sin, convinces us of our need for a Savior, and so prepares us for the proclamation of the Gospel. The Law has this preparatory purpose both historically and experientially. Third, the Gospel takes *precedence in its experienced blessings.* The Law leaves us uncertain at best and in misery and despair at worst. Through the Gospel comes the Spirit with His blessed fruit (5:22–26) and the power of the Word (vv. 2, 5). Finally, the Gospel takes *precedence in its effect.* The Law can convict and condemn, but it cannot save (vv. 10–11). Liberation from sin and death comes only through the Gospel of Jesus, received by faith (vv. 26–29). If we are to be saved, we must flee from the Law to the Gospel.

How foolish to choose bondage to the Law in preference to the freedom and life offered by the Gospel. To do so is actually going backward in God's plan of salvation.

The Prayer Pray today, praising and thanking the Lord for the Gospel and asking for the Spirit's power to believe and live by it.

The Insight First, the Good News.

Week Eleven

Saturday

CIRCUMCISION

The Light **What purpose** did circumcision serve?

Read Genesis 17.

Lord made a covenant with Abram that drew this man and his descendants apart and consecrated them for the sake of "all peoples on earth" (Gen. 12:2–3). This covenant was based solely on God's promise to make Abram a great nation under His special protection for the sake of all nations and to settle them in their own land (Gen. 15:18–21). Abram's part in the covenant was merely to believe the promise God had made; believing would be enough. Abram's trust in that promise from God made him righteous (Gen. 15:6). As a mark of this covenant based on God's promise to bless all peoples through Abram's family, the Lord commanded Abram and all the males among his descendants to be circumcised. Ishmael, Abram's son through Sarai's Egyptian maid Hagar, was not to be the channel through which the covenant of promise would be carried forward; yet he also was circumcised to show that he and his descendants would, through faith in the promise, benefit from it.

The Way **As Paul points out** to the Galatians, God's promise (of which circumcision was the sign) looked ahead to and was fulfilled by the Gospel of Jesus Christ (Gal. 3:16–18). Though circumcision preceded and was distinct from the Law covenant God made through Moses at Sinai, Moses affirmed circumcision and commanded it (Lev. 12:3; John 7:22). But he stressed that the goal and purpose of circumcision is faith (Deut. 10:16; 30:6), and he firmly anchored it in God's work and promise. (Jesus equated circumcision with healing in John 7:23.)

Now that the Lord has fulfilled the promise to which circumcision pointed, fulfilling it by redeeming the world through Jesus (John 3:16), circumcision's role has been completed and no longer has value (Gal. 5:6; 6:15). To insist on circumcision because of its Old Testament command denies that Jesus is the fulfillment of God's promise (Gal. 6:12). In place of circumcision the Lord has given us Holy Baptism as the saving sign of the new covenant based on Christ (Gal. 3:26; Col. 2:11–12).

The Prayer **Pray today,** thanking God for the promise of forgiveness and salvation made to you in Holy Baptism.

The Insight **Store in your memory** this passage: "You are all sons of God through faith in Christ Jesus, for all of you who were baptized into Christ have clothed yourselves with Christ" (Gal. 3:26–27).

Week Twelve

CONTRASTS

The Light How does Paul underscore the Christian's freedom from the burden of the Law's demands?

Read Galatians 4.

Paul contrasts the slavery the Galatians had once experienced—and to which they were considering returning—to the freedom that is theirs through the Gospel of Christ. He first illustrates from experience. He compares their life before they came to faith in Christ with the lot of a minor child who has inherited an estate that he may not claim until he has come of age. They had been subject to "the basic principles of the world." (The exact meaning of this phrase is debated; perhaps Paul refers to their previous subjection to the futility and fatal consequences of sin described in Rom. 5:12–14.) But now through faith in Christ, they have come into their majority and enjoy full access to their inheritance. Do they wish to return to their previous state? Paul uses another illustration from the Old Testament. He recalls that Abraham had two sons, Ishmael and Isaac; the status of these two differed greatly. Isaac, the son of Abraham's proper wife, was to be his heir and carry forward the promise of a Savior. Ishmael, born of a slave woman, had no such blessing. Which son of Abraham did the Galatians wish to be? By faith in the Gospel they had become Abraham's heirs. Did they wish to renounce that inheritance and be cast out with Ishmael?

The Way Paul contrasts the Galatians' present with their former status. Once minor children (v. 3), or even worse, slaves (v. 8) with no hope of an inheritance, they (and we also) are now sons with full rights, heirs who may address the Father with the familiar *Abba*. This word in Aramaic (the tongue spoken in ordinary conversation by Jews in the first century) has a tone of affection and intimacy.

"It was because of an illness that I first preached the gospel to you" (v. 13). We are uninformed of the circumstances to which Paul alludes here or whether the illness is in any way connected to the "thorn in my flesh" to which he refers in 2 Cor. 12:7–10. Whatever it was, this illness apparently detained Paul, providing the opportunity to preach to them. Though a burden on the Galatians, Paul's illness did not put them off.

The Prayer Pray today for persons who are tempted to abandon Christianity for another religion, that God might preserve them in faith.

The Insight The devil pulls us backward, but God moves us forward.

Week Twelve

Tuesday

LIVE FREE!

The Light **What does** Christian freedom mean for us in relation to the Law? What does Christian freedom mean for us in regard to our behavior?

Read Galatians 5.

Christ has made us free from the obligation to keep the Law in order to be just before God. "Christ redeemed us from the curse of the law by becoming a curse for us" (3:13). The Lord has prepared another way of salvation for us—through faith in the work of Christ on our behalf. Since this is so, reobligating ourselves to the Law denies the work of Christ and insults the heavenly Father. "You who are trying to be justified by law have been alienated from Christ; you have fallen away from grace" (5:4). We do not please God by trying hard to keep the Law or by doing the best we can. We please God when we trust Christ's work alone to make us right before His judgment seat. We are free from obligation to the Law. Stand clear of it, and live free!

The Way **We are free** to respond to the Lord's grace. We may use our freedom to "serve one another in love" (v. 13). In this way we obey God's will freely and in freedom fulfill the Law's intent. Such a way of life becomes possible when we "live by the Spirit" (v. 16), responding gladly to His prompting and exhibiting the signs of His presence within us. God now regards our sinful human nature and its behavior as part of our past, a past that was judged and condemned on the cross of Christ. Look back to the cross in gratitude and faith; look to the Christ, who there bore our sins. Then look to the present, to the new self raised with Christ and led by the Spirit. No law regulates the response of the new self. The Law limits, but there can be no limit to love, joy, peace, patience, kindness, gentleness, or self-control.

The Prayer **Pray today** for a greater display of the fruits of the Spirit in your life.

The Insight **"A Christian** is a perfectly free lord of all, subject to none. A Christian is a perfectly dutiful servant of all, subject to all" (Martin Luther, *The Freedom of a Christian*).

Week Twelve

Wednesday

SPIRITUAL LIVING

The Light — **What examples** of spiritual living does Paul provide in the first half of this chapter?

Read Galatians 6.

Before concluding his letter with a summary in verses 11–18, Paul completes his exhortation regarding the free Christian life. Though free from an obligation to be justified through keeping the Law, a Christian voluntarily serves others, just as Christ also "did not come to be served, but to serve, and to give his life as a ransom for many" (Matt. 20:28). While we cannot and need not offer the sacrifice for sin that Jesus did, the Lord commands us to follow His example of service. (See John 13:1–17.) Paul in Gal. 6:1–10 suggests some specific forms this service might take—a humble and gentle spiritual care of others, a sharing in their burdens (vv. 1–5); a generous support of those who teach and minister in the church (v. 6); and an eager alertness to opportunities to do good for others, especially to brothers and sisters in Christ.

The Way — **A good impression** was the goal of those who tried to persuade the Galatians to be circumcised. Whom were they trying to impress? Since Judaism was a tolerated religion within the Roman Empire, perhaps these Judaizing Christians wanted to "look Jewish" and thus avoid suspicion and possible persecution from Gentiles. More likely, they feared rejection and persecution from Jews, their "parent" religion. Whatever the motivation, seeking to escape persecution by giving up the Gospel is no option for Christians. For in Christ, crucified for our sins and raised for our justification, we have all that is worth our living, suffering, and dying.

"I bear on my body the marks of Jesus" (v. 17). Paul proudly owned the scars resulting from his suffering for the Lord as proof that he belonged to Christ. Is there anything about us that marks us as belonging to the Lord?

The Prayer — **Pray today** for a greater awareness that you belong to Christ.

The Insight — **Better a cross** with Christ than no cross of Christ.

78

EPHESIANS

Christians who have read the New Testament often and thoroughly likely have a special place in their hearts for this letter. Other letters of Paul (such as Corinthians and Galatians) were occasioned by problems or looming threats, but the letter to the Ephesians is positive and celebrative throughout. Even though Paul wrote this letter (together with Colossians and Philemon) while imprisoned, his mood is optimistic and confident.

Ephesians, a valuable source of teaching, delineates the doctrine of the church. Here we learn the church's *essence* and how we as members are related to one another.

If one key word of this epistle is *church,* another is *peace.* Paul reminds us that Christ our Savior is the source of our peace, and that our fellowship with one another in the church is a fellowship of peace.

Ephesians continues to fulfill the purpose for which it was first written: to strengthen and build up Christ's church in love and peace.

GOD'S GRAND PLAN

The Light What grand plan of God does Paul explain in this first chapter? How does the exposition of this plan encourage Christians?

Read Ephesians 1.

Paul visited Ephesus during his second missionary tour and then spent two years proclaiming the Gospel in Ephesus (Acts 19:10) during his third tour. On his way to Rome, though he did not pass through Ephesus, he consulted the pastors of the Ephesian church. In view of Paul's long stay in this major eastern Mediterranean port city and capitol of the Roman province of Asia (today, western Turkey), the letter of Paul "to the saints in Ephesus" seems somewhat out of character. Strangely, Paul says he has not stopped giving thanks "ever since I *heard* about your faith in the Lord Jesus and your love for all the saints" (v. 15)—an unusual comment if Paul's knowledge of the congregation had been personal. But the letter gives no indication that Paul personally knew the recipients, and he conveys no personal greetings or references, as he customarily did. (See Rom. 16; 1 Cor. 16:5–24; Phil. 4:2–3, 14, 21–22; Col. 4:7–18.) Plus, the earliest copies of this letter do not have the words "in Ephesus" in verse 1, and the title "To the Ephesians" was not appended until later. Therefore, many scholars, both ancient and modern, believe the letter was written to churches in neighboring cities such as Colossae, Laodicea, and Hierapolis, and that this circular letter was preserved in Ephesus, taking on its name. Some believe the letter possessed by the Laodiceans (Col. 4:16) is actually our "Ephesians."

The Way Whether or not Paul personally knew those to whom he wrote this letter, the *Lord* knew them. From eternity He had predestined them for salvation. He caused the Gospel to be proclaimed to them and gave them the Holy Spirit, who enabled them to believe (vv. 11–14). This encourages all of Paul's readers—including us. God has chosen us, called us, and keeps us in faith. This truth gives us great confidence as we struggle to remain faithful. God will not let us go!

Paul prayed that his readers might know Christ better (vv. 17–19). That is also the goal for us as we grow together in Christian knowledge and faith.

The Prayer Pray today for a growing understanding and appreciation of God's grace in Christ.

The Insight God counts even new Christians as old friends.

Week Twelve

Friday

BEFORE AND AFTER

The Light What changes had occurred in the lives of Paul's readers when they became Christians?

Read Ephesians 2.

Those who received this letter were Gentiles. Before coming to faith in Christ they had been "dead in ... transgressions and sins," had "followed the ways of this world and of the ruler of the kingdom of the air, the spirit who is now at work in those who are disobedient" (vv. 1–2). They were totally under the control of Satan, who is the "prince of this world" (John 12:31; 14:30; 16:11). As Gentiles they were excluded from God's kingdom, "separate from Christ, excluded from citizenship in Israel and foreigners to the covenants of the promise, without hope and without God in the world" (v. 12). But what a change has occurred! Now God has "made us alive with Christ ... raised us up with Christ and seated us with him in the heavenly realms in Christ Jesus ... by grace ... not by works" (vv. 5–6, 8, 9). Furthermore, God has now made us "fellow citizens with God's people and members of God's household, built on the foundation of the apostles and prophets, with Christ Jesus himself as the chief cornerstone" (vv. 19–20).

The Way Not only does faith in Christ unite us with Him, but it also takes down walls separating us from other people. The Lord had once commanded Israel to separate from other peoples (1 Kings 8:53; Ezra 10:11) for the sake of its mission—to bring forth the promised Seed of Abraham for the salvation of the nations. But now that mission is done, and the Lord "has destroyed the barrier, the dividing wall of hostility, by abolishing in His flesh the law with its commandments and regulations" (vv. 14–15). Since Jews and Gentiles alike are reconciled to God "through the cross," they are also to be reconciled to one another by the same cross.

What is true of Jews and Gentiles is also true of other individuals and groups separated by suspicion, hatred, ignorance, or other barriers. We all come together before the cross of Jesus.

The Prayer Pray today for someone whom you believe to be still "dead in ... transgressions" and "without hope and without God in the world," that God might save that person by grace through Christ.

The Insight The cross stands on common ground.

81

Week Twelve

SEPARATED FOR A PURPOSE

The Light Why was Ezra distressed when he discovered that Israelite men had married non-Israelite women?

Read Ezra 9–10.

God had forbidden the Israelites to intermarry with the peoples they would find in the Promised Land. In 9:11–12, Ezra summarizes such passages as Ex. 34:11–16 and Deut. 7:1–4. Israel's separation from other peoples was no narrow-minded chauvinism. God had selected Israel as the nation that would produce the world's Savior. For Israel's sake, as well as for the nations from which they were separated, Israel was not to be drawn away from its dedication to the Lord or from the role He had given it. But Israel *had* broken the Lord's command and *had* fallen into the worst forms of apostasy and idolatry. It had not remained a light to the nations but had forsaken its light and fled into the darkness of gross iniquities, taking part in horribly corrupt practices that God detested. Rather than destroy the nation utterly, the Lord submitted Israel to a drastic cleansing—the destruction of Jerusalem and the exile of its people in Babylon, from which a mere remnant emerged. Even this harsh punishment displayed God's mercy toward Israel and His determination to complete His plan of grace.

The Way Ezra openly offered a fervent prayer and an anguished confession that implicated the entire surviving nation in the guilt brought about by the offenses of some. His public grief alarmed those who witnessed it and moved them to pledge their support if Ezra would only act quickly and decisively to remove the grave crisis. God has often raised up spiritual leaders who are able to bring about a public movement of repentance, revival, and renewal.

Sometimes one individual's crime brings shame and hurt on many others. But the Savior's shame and hurt made healing and salvation available to all.

The Prayer Pray today that you may live consistent with God's purpose for you as His witness.

The Insight Store in your memory this passage: "Because of his great love for us, God, who is rich in mercy, made us alive with Christ even when we were dead in transgressions—it is by grace you have been saved" (Eph. 2:4–5).

Week Thirteen

Monday

A MYSTERY REVEALED

The Light What is the mystery of which Paul speaks in this chapter?

Read Ephesians 3.

Ephesians, Philippians, Colossians, and Philemon are referred to as the "Captivity Letters" by New Testament scholars. They apparently were sent while Paul was a prisoner in Rome during the period described in Acts 28:30–31. While a prisoner (v. 1), Paul was able to receive visitors and to send correspondence, and in this way he continued to attend to the needs of the churches. Even though his situation involved sufferings (v. 13), he viewed his position as God-given and accepted it with patience. Though confined by chains, Paul was yet able to proclaim the Gospel with the hope that God might open doors for its reception (Col. 4:3). He hoped to be released and allowed to revisit the area to which he now wrote (Philemon 22).

The Way This *mystery*—Paul repeatedly uses this term in chapter 1 (v. 9), four times in this chapter (vv. 3, 4, 6, 9), and once each in chapters 5 (v. 32) and 6 (v. 19). In other letters, *mystery* appears in Romans twice (11:25 and 16:25), in 1 Corinthians twice (2:7 and 15:51), in Colossians four times (1:26, 27; 2:2; 4:3), in 2 Thessalonians once (2:7), and in 1 Timothy twice (3:9, 16). In Scripture, a *mystery* is a truth unknowable to the human mind apart from revelation by God. In Ephesians and most other uses by Paul, the *mystery* is the Gospel. This Gospel is available also to Gentiles. Although Paul did not by any means minister exclusively to Gentiles (nor did the other apostles minister exclusively to Jews), he regarded the ministry of revealing the mystery of the Gospel to the Gentiles as a grace given especially to him.

Paul prays fervently, kneeling before the Father (v. 14) on behalf of his flock. Do we pray fervently, imploring God's grace on behalf of others?

The Prayer Pray today for some person in your family or church, that he or she might grow in Christian knowledge, faith, and love.

The Insight God's mystery is no longer a secret.

Week Thirteen

Tuesday

CHURCH LIFE

The Light What connection does Paul make between the Christian's calling and the Christian's life?

Read Ephesians 4.

In Ephesians Paul emphasizes that the holy Christian church is the body of Christ and the communion of saints. Paul strikes the keynote of his instruction regarding the church in the doxology at the end of chapter 3 ("to him be glory in the church and in Christ Jesus"). References to the church are peppered throughout the epistle. But in chapter 4, Paul zeroes in on the essence of the church. A series of seven "ones" (one body, one Spirit, one hope, one Lord, one faith, one baptism, one God and Father of all) emphasizes the unity of the church—a unity created and preserved by God. To serve this unity, God has given a diversity of ministries (apostles, prophets, evangelists, pastors and teachers) "to prepare God's people for works of service" and to bring them to a mature knowledge of God's will. Sound teaching fosters the unity of the church as it cultivates among Christians the sure and certain foundation of faith in Christ, the Head of the church.

The Way Church life centers in the community gathered around Christ. The life of the church emanates from that center through its members into the world. Here Christians exhibit a way of life greatly different from those who are separated from God and live in the darkness of sin. Christians are "new"— "new in the attitude of your minds" and with a "new self, created to be like God in true righteousness and holiness." Their newness is apparent in their truthfulness, honesty, generosity, wholesomeness, peaceableness, kindness, compassion, and Christlike forgiveness.

Grown-up Christians—mature in their thinking and stable in their reactions to what they hear, see, and experience—are the Spirit's goal for the nurture that takes place in the church. God means for you to grow up in every respect, also in your faith.

The Prayer Pray today for those who serve your church as educators, both as professionals and volunteers, that their efforts may strengthen your congregation's unity and stability through the Gospel.

The Insight You too are new through Christ.

Week Thirteen

Wednesday

CHILDREN OF LIGHT

The Light

In what arenas of life are Christians to be children of light?

Read Ephesians 5.

Like our own society—in some respects, at least—society in the first century after Christ showed alarming signs of moral decay. This was evident especially in sexual immorality. Licentiousness could be found on every level of society, beginning in the imperial palaces at Rome. Sexual immorality often included perversions such as homosexuality and sex with children. Paul was not exaggerating when he wrote of many in his day: "Having lost all sensitivity, they have given themselves over to sensuality so as to indulge in every kind of impurity, with a continual lust for more" (4:19). Such moral decadence was actually fostered by *heathen religions* in which sexual sins were encouraged and practiced. The gods and goddesses worshiped in the temples were hardly examples of moral restraint. All of this influenced *family life*. Divorce was common, and relationships between children and parents were often marked by disrespect and disharmony.

The Way

In such a context Christians stand out as "light in the Lord." They strive to live in the world free of "even a hint of sexual immorality, or of any kind of impurity, or of greed, because these are improper for God's holy people." Not only in actions but in talk they avoid obscenity, foolishness, and coarse joking. Instead, they speak words of thanksgiving. They desire to "find out what pleases the Lord." Christian worship encourages such godly behavior, for Christ's people "speak to one another with psalms, hymns and spiritual songs" and "sing and make music in your heart to the Lord, always giving thanks." The Christian marriage and family mirrors Christ's own relationship to the church, characterized by mutual love and devotion.

All this is possible because the Spirit of God is present and working through the Gospel.

The Prayer

Pray today, yielding to God the Holy Spirit a larger place in your own life so your life in Christ might be light in society, church, and family.

The Insight

Christians gleam in the gloom.

Week Thirteen

FULLY ARMED

The Light Who supplies what Christians need to fulfill their duties successfully?

Read Ephesians 6.

Reverence for Christ as Lord moves Christians to fulfill the roles God has given in this life. Christian wives submit to their husbands and in this way reverence Christ. Christian husbands are devoted to their wives and in this way mirror Christ. Christian children obey and honor their parents and in this way obey and honor their heavenly Father. Christian parents bring up their children with patience and bring them to the Lord through His Word and in this way share with their children their chief treasure. Christians who are under the direction of others serve wholeheartedly and in this way serve Christ the Lord. Christians who direct the work of others do so with respectful consideration and in this way display brotherhood and a hope common to all. Christ at the center gives all our relationships new meaning, dignity, and importance.

The Way Christian living requires a strength of purpose and perseverance that we, in ourselves, do not have. God supplies the defensive armor and the offensive weapons that are required to resist the hostile spiritual forces that would otherwise soon overpower us. Paul checks off each piece of equipment that the Lord issues to his soldiers, finding a spiritual counterpart to each item of military gear. (Perhaps Paul had such a soldier before his eyes as he wrote—Acts 28:16). The equipment of which Paul speaks is the Lord's own, which He now issues to us. (See Is. 11:5; 49:2; 59:17.)

In addition, the Lord gives us the power of prayer, which He intends that we use by praying for others (Eph. 6:18–20). Do we most often pray for ourselves—or for others, as the Lord intends?

The Prayer Pray today for someone you know who needs God's help and encouragement as a witness to the Gospel.

The Insight Christian soldiers are "G.I.s"—our equipment is *God's Issue.*

86

Week Thirteen

Friday

THE LORD'S SERVANT

The Light

What problem does Jude address in this letter?

Read Jude.

James and Jude were the natural brothers of Jesus. Mentioned in Matt. 13:55 and Mark 6:3, they at first failed to accept Jesus as the Messiah (Mark 3:21, 31–35). They are not mentioned as present at Jesus' crucifixion, where the Lord entrusted his mother to John (John 19:26–27). But after Jesus' resurrection we find them in the company of the church (Acts 1:14), and they became active as Christian missionaries (1 Cor. 9:5). James (to be distinguished from the apostle James, the son of Zebedee and the brother of John the apostle, and from James the son of Alphaeus, another of Jesus' disciples) became leader of the church at Jerusalem (Acts 15:13; Gal. 1:19; 2:9); he is the author of the epistle of James. Neither James nor Jude refer to themselves—nor does anyone else refer to them—as apostles. Though Paul (and no doubt others) referred to them as "the Lord's brothers," neither James nor Jude claim this distinction for themselves (James 1:1; Jude 1); they are simply Jesus' servants. They were willing to acknowledge that Jesus' brothers and sisters are all those who believe in him.

The Way

Though preferring to write in a more positive vein (v. 3), Jude has an unwelcome but essential task: he must warn and admonish the church (which particular congregation or congregations we cannot know) about a grave threat. Certain teachers, claiming to be true Christians (vv. 4, 12), practiced and encouraged sexual license under the guise of Christian liberty (v. 4). In this connection see Gal. 5:13, 19–21. Perhaps they claimed visions and revelations from angels as authorizing their behavior and teaching. But Jude counters their claims with many Biblical references and examples. He also cites two writings not in the Bible—the Book of Enoch (Jude 14–15 and perhaps also v. 6) and The Assumption of Moses (now mostly lost to us) in verse 9. Though unusual, Jude's use of writings from outside the Bible is not unique; Paul quotes three Greek poets: Menander (in 1 Cor. 15:33), Epimenides (Titus 1:12; Acts 17:28a), and Aratus (Acts 17:28b). These references by Paul and Jude do not, of course, imply that these non-Biblical writings were inspired by the Holy Spirit.

Purity of faith and life is Jude's goal for Christians, and he urges us to adopt that same goal for ourselves and others. Christ died to make us pure before God. May we share Jude's earnest concern that we retain such purity.

The Prayer

Pray today that God might preserve the church from error in faith and life.

The Insight

License is to liberty what leering is to looking.

87

A FAITHFUL WOMAN

The Light How is Ruth a model for us in our family relationships?

Read Ruth.

Why is Ruth's story chosen by the Holy Spirit for inclusion in Holy Scripture? Perhaps because, as the great-grandmother of King David and an ancestress of Jesus Christ (Matt. 1:5), she holds a place of honor in Biblical history. But this in itself hardly answers the question; the story of other ancestors is not included. Rather, Ruth illustrates a faith that results in great faithfulness. No wonder that her words (Ruth 1:16–17) have become a favorite wedding text (though Ruth spoke them to her mother-in-law)! Her loyalty and love for those to whom God had joined her worthily models all our family ties, beginning with marriage but extending also to other relationships—yes, even with in-laws. Ruth lived near the end of the period of the judges. We do not know who recorded for the ages her sweet, inspiring story. Jewish traditions assign authorship to Samuel, though the narrative may well have been written down during the time of David, the last person mentioned in the book.

The Way What accounted for Ruth's remarkable loyalty to Naomi, that quality that first attracted admiration and inspired love for her in her future husband (2:11–12)? Both Ruth and Orpah clearly loved their mother-in-law, who was herself a considerate and intelligent woman. But we may also believe that Ruth had come to a true and persisting faith in the God of Israel as the only God (1:16; 2:12). We may also conclude that Ruth had come to know and trust in the promises God had made concerning the Savior—promises God would bring to fulfillment partly through her.

Not an Israelite by birth, Ruth represents the Gentile world that the Savior, her own descendant, would also redeem. The Lord also came for us and chooses to work through us.

The Prayer Pray today that God might give you a love and loyalty for your family members like that of Ruth for Naomi.

The Insight Store in your memory this passage: "Submit to one another out of reverence for Christ"(Eph. 5:21).

New Testament Timeline

[Note: Although some events can be accurately dated, we must use deduction and conjecture to construct a complete New Testament timeline.]

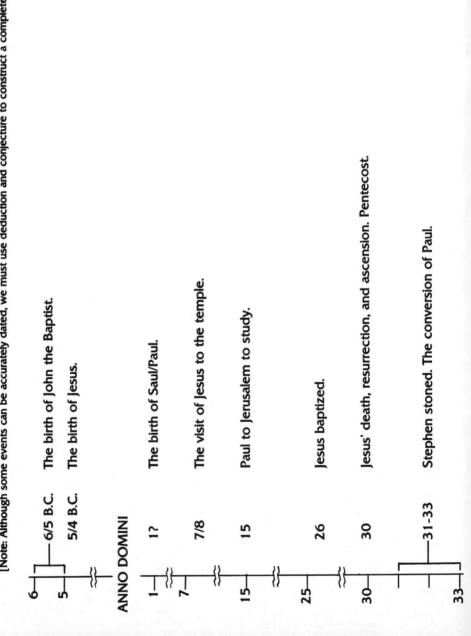

6/5 B.C.	The birth of John the Baptist.
5/4 B.C.	The birth of Jesus.

ANNO DOMINI

1?	The birth of Saul/Paul.
7/8	The visit of Jesus to the temple.
15	Paul to Jerusalem to study.
26	Jesus baptized.
30	Jesus' death, resurrection, and ascension. Pentecost.
31-33	Stephen stoned. The conversion of Paul.

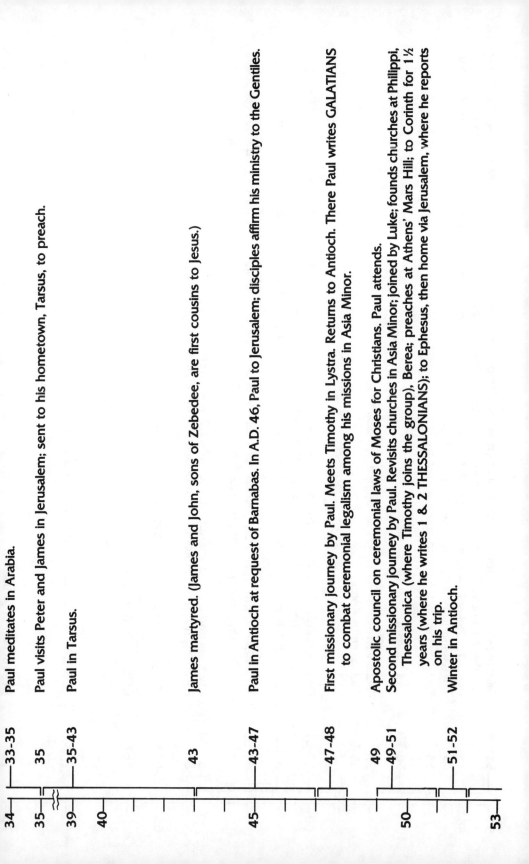

34		
33-35	Paul meditates in Arabia.
35	Paul visits Peter and James in Jerusalem; sent to his hometown, Tarsus, to preach.
35-43	Paul in Tarsus.
43	James martyred. (James and John, sons of Zebedee, are first cousins to Jesus.)
43-47	Paul in Antioch at request of Barnabas. In A.D. 46, Paul to Jerusalem; disciples affirm his ministry to the Gentiles.
47-48	First missionary journey by Paul. Meets Timothy in Lystra. Returns to Antioch. There Paul writes GALATIANS to combat ceremonial legalism among his missions in Asia Minor.
49	Apostolic council on ceremonial laws of Moses for Christians. Paul attends.
49-51	Second missionary journey by Paul. Revisits churches in Asia Minor; joined by Luke; founds churches at Philippi, Thessalonica (where Timothy joins the group), Berea; preaches at Athens' Mars Hill; to Corinth for 1½ years (where he writes 1 & 2 THESSALONIANS); to Ephesus, then home via Jerusalem, where he reports on his trip.
51-52	Winter in Antioch.
53	

Date	Event
52-56	Third missionary journey by Paul. Brief stops in Asia Minor, then 2 years, 3 months in Ephesus. Probably founds the 7 churches listed in Revelation. Shortly before leaving Ephesus, wrote 1 CORINTHIANS. To Philippi (where he wrote 2 CORINTHIANS); to Thessalonica, Berea, 3 months in Corinth (while writing ROMANS); and back to Jerusalem to report.
56	Paul Arrested in Jerusalem. Interrogated by Felix at Caesarea.
56-58	Paul imprisoned at Caesarea.
58	Paul, interrogated by Festus & Agrippa, appeals to Rome.
58-59	Paul taken to Rome.
59-61	Paul's first Roman imprisonment, awaiting trial. ACTS probably written at this time, by Luke. Paul probably here wrote the "captivity letters": PHILEMON, COLOSSIANS, EPHESIANS, and PHILIPPIANS.
61-64?	JAMES, JUDE (by Jesus' brothers) and THE LETTERS OF PETER probably written during these years.
61-63	A possible fourth missionary journey by Paul—to Spain, Crete (appoints Titus pastor), Ephesus (appoints Timothy pastor), to Philippi (where he writes 1 TIMOTHY and TITUS), and back to Rome.
63-64	Paul's second imprisonment in Rome; writes 2 TIMOTHY.
64	Following major fire in Rome, Nero persecutes the church.
65?	Martyrdom of St. Paul. Probably St. Peter also.
66?	GOSPEL OF MARK written.
?	HEBREWS written before the fall of Jerusalem.
70	Destruction of Jerusalem

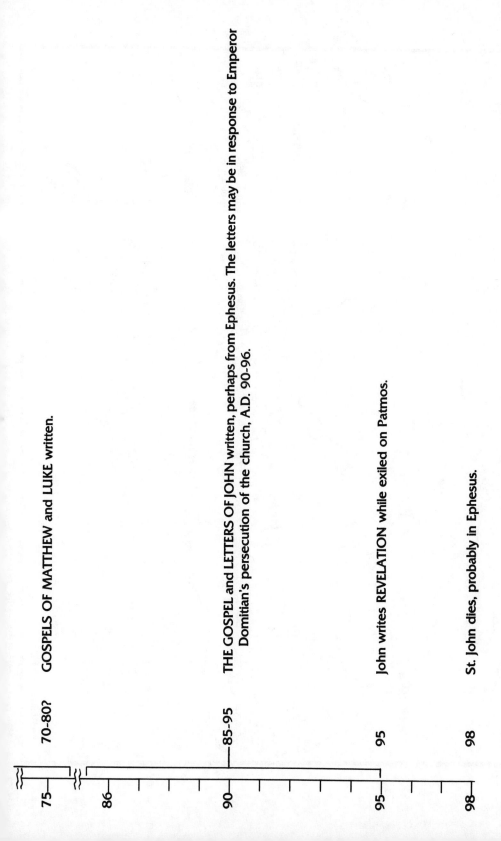

70-80?   GOSPELS OF MATTHEW and LUKE written.

85-95   THE GOSPEL and LETTERS OF JOHN written, perhaps from Ephesus. The letters may be in response to Emperor Domitian's persecution of the church, A.D. 90-96.

95   John writes REVELATION while exiled on Patmos.

98   St. John dies, probably in Ephesus.

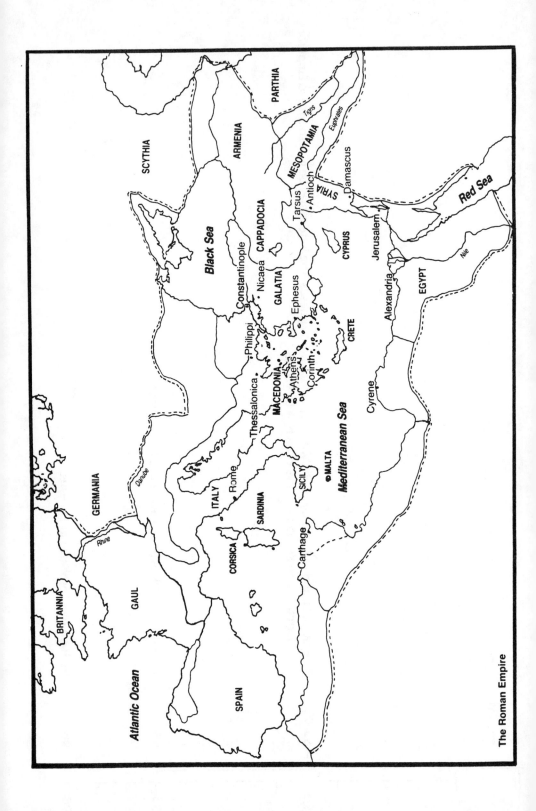

The Roman Empire

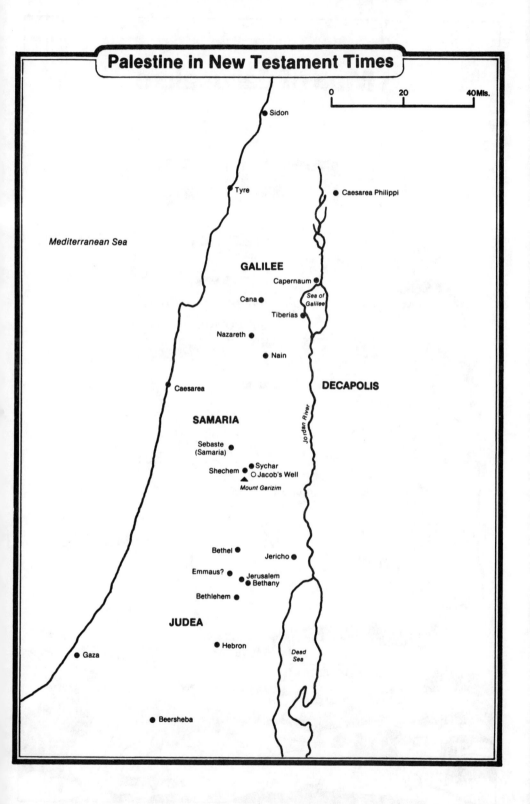

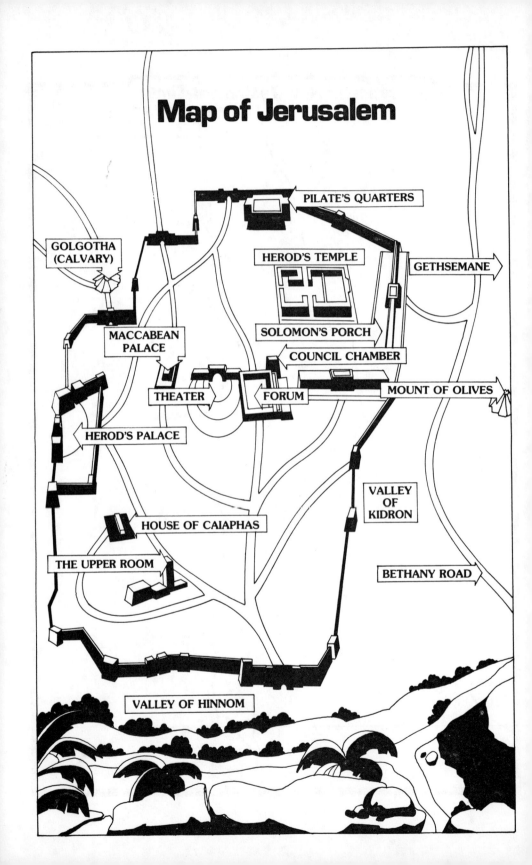

Map of Jerusalem

PILATE'S QUARTERS

GOLGOTHA (CALVARY)

HEROD'S TEMPLE

GETHSEMANE

MACCABEAN PALACE

SOLOMON'S PORCH

COUNCIL CHAMBER

THEATER

FORUM

MOUNT OF OLIVES

HEROD'S PALACE

VALLEY OF KIDRON

HOUSE OF CAIAPHAS

THE UPPER ROOM

BETHANY ROAD

VALLEY OF HINNOM